11-12-68

Reprints of Economic Classics

MODERN CAPITALISM

Also Published in

REPRINTS OF ECONOMIC CLASSICS

By Henri See

The Economic Interpretation of History [1929]

Sans estude et sans art, tu decides en maistre,
Et tes decisions sont pleines d'Equité.
Son Livre Sert de Regle, et fait assez connaistre,
Ce que peut le bon Sens; joint a la probité.

Carpel pinxit pinxit   Edelinck Sculp. CPR.

MODERN CAPITALISM

Its Origin and Evolution

By

HENRI SÉE

Honorary Professor, University of Rennes

Translated by

HOMER B. VANDERBLUE

Professor of Business Economics

and

GEORGES F. DORIOT

Associate Professor of Manufacturing

Graduate School of Business Administration
Harvard University

George F. Baker Foundation

Reprints of Economic Classics

AUGUSTUS M. KELLEY PUBLISHERS

New York 1968

First Edition 1928

(New York: Adelphi Company, 1928)

Reprinted 1968 by
AUGUSTUS M. KELLEY · PUBLISHERS
NEW YORK NEW YORK 10010

LIBRARY OF CONGRESS CATALOGUE CARD NUMBER

67 - 30864

PRINTED IN THE UNITED STATES OF AMERICA
by SENTRY PRESS, NEW YORK, N. Y. 10019

1476037

CONTENTS

CHAPTER I

CHAPTER II

CHAPTER III

CHAPTER IV

CHAPTER V

CHAPTER VI

CHAPTER VII

CONTENTS vii

CONTENTS

CHAPTER XI

LIST OF ILLUSTRATIONS

ix

FOREWORD

The original volume of which this book is a translation is at once remarkable for its charming style and for the author's brilliant achievement in presenting the results of extended researches within brief compass. In two hundred pages of a little volume which slips readily into one's pocket, Professor Sée has created a fascinating survey of the rise of capitalism. Its origins he finds in the commercial activities of the Mediterranean world; and he traces its spread over Europe and America through the channels of trade and finance, as no one has done before him. What he so aptly calls commercial capitalism and financial capitalism were the necessary precursors of industrial capitalism, the third stage in the evolution of modern capitalism. Today we have a union of all three.

Naturally, then, the greatest virtue of Professor Sée's book —aside from its simple style,—is due to his skill in picking out and assembling significant bits of evidence from an amazing variety of materials. Here his success bespeaks the unusual scholar, fully experienced in making detailed historical researches on his own account. Professor Sée possesses an almost uncanny ability to pick out essentials, to discard nonessentials, and to draw significant conclusions. In these particulars, this essay is a masterly example of the historian's art.[1]

Over thirty-five years of study have gone into its making. Professor Sée served as Professor of Modern History at the University of Rennes from 1893 until his retirement in 1920. Immediately upon taking up residence at Rennes, he began researches, the finest fruits of which are only now being pub-

[1] For a more extended (and most enthusiastic) appraisal of this book, see Professor Melvin M. Knight's review, *The Quarterly Journal of Economics*, May 1927, p. 520.

lished. His earlier works were concerned mainly with the materials which he found close at hand: for, above all, Professor Sée is the economic historian of Brittany. The leisure which has accrued since his retirement in 1920 has been used in bringing out, in rapid succession, a brilliant series of works on economic history. These are at once the fruits of careful and extended researches and of well considered reflection.

The present volume is, then, but one of several outstanding works of Professor Sée to appear recently. It is, no doubt, the volume most likely to appeal to American readers generally; and on this account Professor Doriot and I were the more easily tempted to undertake the task of translation. But English editions of other of Professor Sée's recent works have already appeared or are promised, including his important study of agrarian history (*Esquisse d'une histoire du régime agraire en Europe aux XVIIIe et XIXe siècles*), which received the Gabriel Monod Prize of the Institute of France in 1922, and his most recent work on *The Science and Philosophy of History*. In the latter work, he develops at length his theories of historical method,—theories which, especially as they are related to the task immediately in hand, are presented much more briefly in the preface to this volume.

In conclusion, I must express again what I have expressed in my correspondence with Professor Sée—an acknowledgement of gratitude for his patient and sympathetic cooperation in our work. I am greatly indebted to Miss Alice M. Belcher to whom I have turned from time to time for assistance in clearing up obscurities in the translation, and to Miss E. F. Philbrook who has helped with the reading of the proof. Miss Edna B. Allen has prepared the index.

HOMER B. VANDERBLUE.

Glass Hall
Soldiers Field
March, 1928

PREFACE

This English translation of my volume *Les origines du capitalisme moderne*, which originally appeared in 1926 in the Armand Colin Collection, is, in many respects, a second edition. Since publication of that volume, new works bearing on the subject have appeared, and I have perceived certain gaps in my own presentation. Furthermore, I have recognized as just certain suggestions and observations of competent critics both in France and abroad; and I have endeavored to take such into account. Therefore additional and supplementary materials, new references, and a somewhat fuller bibliography appear in this English edition.

Nevertheless, the volume preserves its original character. It is neither a manual nor a summary, but rather a synthetic sketch of a very vast subject, which would demand a number of volumes for its complete treatment. Such elaborate treatment, of necessity, should be based on innumerable intensive monographs, and most of these—unfortunately—are yet to be written. There is no phenomenon more international in its scope than capitalism, even in the period when its existence and influence were still barely evident; and there is no field of investigation where the comparative method can be employed more usefully, where workers of all countries can collaborate more effectively, or where the possibilities of international collaboration can be more clearly visualized. The present volume may well prove useful as a sort of introduction to this kind of study; and I hope it may stimulate students of economic and social history—and even historians in general—to new labors in this broad field of investigation.

And perhaps economists, also, may use this volume to some

advantage; for political economy has recently been turning more and more to a consideration of historical materials. In general, however, political economy undertakes to study the production, distribution, and consumption of wealth, without taking great account of those contingencies with which history must be concerned. This statement should not be understood as meaning that the historian does not receive great help from the company of sociologists and economists. Are not the latter concerned mainly with observing contemporaneous society? And the historian, in order to understand the past, needs to know and to understand the present. Would it occur to us to study the genesis of capitalism if we did not live in a society characterized by a capitalistic organization?

The present sketch is not meant as a general history of modern capitalism, however; and still less have I attempted to write a sociological essay. Nor can this modest study in any way pretend to rival the monumental work of Professor Werner Sombart, *Der moderne Kapitalismus*—a volume remarkable for its vast, albeit sometimes slightly confused, erudition and especially remarkable for the very suggestive and striking opinions set forth. On the contrary, it has been my intention simply to assemble and to synthesize conclusions drawn from a variety of generally accepted historical data, data chosen with a view to the service they might render to sociology and political economy through elucidating the origins of capitalism. Thus, in a word, the present study has been projected as an essay of synthesis and comparative history, undertaken without any political or social bias. I have endeavored to give an account of the great economic and social evolution which ended in the triumph of capitalism and large scale industry during the nineteenth century.

In this connection, it is important to indicate my methods of study and presentation. Though the aim has been to make certain historical materials available to students of sociology and political economy, yet I have been very careful not to

borrow from the methods of these two sciences in the slight-
est degree; for political economy, in studying the laws of production, distribution, and consumption of wealth, takes but
slight account of "contingencies" (*contingences*); and sociology gives only secondary consideration to time and space; its
main object is to describe the socialized organization *in ab-
stracto*. For the present study, on the other hand, it has been
essential to consider time and space: I have studied capitalism
not merely as a process of evolution extending over a period of
years, but as a phenomenon developing in quite different
regions.

The method most likely to prove fruitful in the sort of
study here attempted is the comparative method. Since the
desire has been to study the origins of capitalism, not in a
single country but everywhere that they might be perceived,
my resort to the method of comparative history has been the
more natural and necessary. What I would call comparisons
in *space* and also in *time* have been made, because the accumulation of capital—the necessary condition of capitalism
—did not take place in the Middle Ages in the same fashion
as in Modern Times. And the capitalistic organization of the
Middle Ages, still sporadic and embryonic, was very different from the organization which came to prevail in the eighteenth and nineteenth centuries. In the main, it is such differences which govern the nature of the evolution of capitalism
and determine the character of modern capitalistic society.

Since this has been projected primarily as an historical
study, I have endeavored always to have recourse to concrete
facts; and yet, since I have aimed at effecting a synthesis and
have of necessity used *generalizations*, all abstraction has not
been avoided, I fear. And yet this result seems to have been
inevitable, for a fairly close connection necessarily exists between generalization and abstraction.

Another disadvantage of such a study as this is that facts
of another order—political, religious, and intellectual facts,

for example—are necessarily relegated to an obscure position, even when, as in many cases, they may well have exercised a notable influence on the genesis of capitalism. Personalities are also left completely in the background; though
they too have had no little influence on the economic evolution here studied. Even if its importance has often been exaggerated, did not Colbert's work, for example, contribute
toward the evolution of capitalism, at least in France?

In a word, all the individual facts, which form the warp
of general history, are sacrificed in such a study as that here
presented, and doubtless excessively so. Yet an essay of synthesis and comparative history can render some service, even
to general history. Does it not explain certain facts of another order more forcibly? Does it not contribute a demon-
stration of the interrelationships of such facts? Doubtless
it may be considered that the *individual* alone corresponds
to the reality; but, since the *general* is more intelligible than
the particular, its study may help us to understand better this
category of facts which have occurred only once in a certain
manner, and which, so long as they remain in scattered sources,
are not readily accessible to science.

Finally, I must express my warmest thanks to Professor
Vanderblue and Professor Doriot for their care and interest in
the work of translation; and especially to the former for his
kindness in adding certain references at appropriate places in
the text, and in completing the list of works in the Bibliography. I am also happy to include Mr. H. T. Warshow in my
expression of gratitude. His friendly diligence has ensured a
perfection to this edition of my volume which can only flat-
ter the *amour propre* of the author.

Henri Sée

Rennes,
December, 1927.

CHAPTER I

INTRODUCTION

A FIRST essential in the study of a subject like the present is a clear understanding of terms. Exactly what is to be understood by the expression: *modern capitalism?* Certain writers have asserted that capitalism originated as soon as mobile wealth had been developed; and, if this definition be accepted, capitalism may be said to have been in existence in the Ancient World, not only in that of the Greeks and Romans, but even farther back in the more ancient societies which carried on active commercial transactions.

But such is a case of purely commercial and financial capitalism, if it be capitalism at all. Capitalism never took hold of industry in the Ancient World; and only small craftsmen, supplying local markets, were to be found at work among the Greeks and even in the Roman world. In the main, slave labor provided for the needs of the household (*familia*) just as it provided for those of the large Roman estates (*latifundia*).

In the first centuries of the Middle Ages, beginning with the time of Charlemagne at least, economic life was almost solely rural in character; the towns were merely fortresses and places of refuge. There was no longer a trace of capitalism. Then the Crusades extended the relations of the Mediterranean countries with the East and thereby stimulated a great commercial expansion enabling the Genoese, the Pisans, and especially the Venetians to accumulate great wealth. This commercial activity accounts for the first manifestations of capitalism in the Italian republics. Yet there was nothing in any way resembling a capitalistic régime, in the modern sense of the word.

Indeed, what are the essential characteristics of capitalistic society, as it exists today? The expansion of international commerce on a large scale is not its sole distinguishing mark; on the contrary, it includes also the flowering of a large scale industry, the triumph of machinery, and the growing power of the great financial houses. In a word, it is the present day *union* of all these phenomena which really constitutes modern capitalism.

Furthermore, the distant origins of this régime do not go back farther than the period when capitalism began to exercise its power over industry in such regions as were active economically, like Italy and the Low Countries in the thirteenth century. In those days, capitalism was mainly, and almost solely, commercial capitalism, though even then it was beginning to reach out and to assume control over industrial activity. But, as the subsequent discussion makes clear, capitalism was still in the stage of its humble beginnings, albeit a new economic force was to be distinguished even at this early period: a movement was under way which was destined, in the end, to stir the whole economic world.

Capital and *capitalism* must be distinguished clearly in order to avoid confusion. When one takes the strictly historical point of view, he is not obliged, as is the economist, to take the word capital in the full breadth of its meaning. No doubt, land and the instruments of production are, like transferable securities, the source of wealth, and in that sense, capital. But whoever attempts to trace the evolution of modern capitalism must seek to trace the history of the great rôle played by capital in the form of transferable securities.

Use of the word *capital* originated fairly late; and the word was first employed to designate a sum designed to be *invested* to bring in an *interest*.[1] Doubtless, use of the word by economists has extended its meaning to cover the concept which has prevailed in economic science.

In reality, capital originated the day when mobile wealth developed, principally in the form of coin. The accumulation of capital was a necessary condition of the genesis of capitalism; and such accumulation became more and more accentuated with the opening of the sixteenth century, though by itself not sufficient to accomplish the formation of a capitalistic society. Capitalism first appeared in the form of commercial capitalism and financial capitalism; before the final evolution could be achieved, further changes must have occurred: there must have been a transformation in the whole organization of labor and in the relations between employers and employees. This transformation produced quite the most profound change in social classes which had yet occurred. Finally, the triumph of capitalistic organization did not come until the nineteenth century; and nearly everywhere, indeed, its final triumph awaited the coming of the second half of that century.

CHAPTER II

THE FIRST MANIFESTATIONS OF CAPITALISM

I. CAPITALISM IN THE ANCIENT WORLD

L ENGTHY discussion of capitalism in ancient times is not worth while, for the documentary evidence is not exact enough to permit such discussion in anything like definite terms. There is, however, one fact which stands out clearly: whereas landed property dominated the economic life of the Roman Empire, as in Greece and the Hellenic states, manufacturing on any considerable scale proved incompatible with a system of household economy in which slave labor played a large part. Trading operations on a large scale, particularly in maritime commerce, were probably not unknown in antiquity, though the importance such commerce attained cannot be estimated with anything like exactness.

In the main, however, the capital fund accumulated out of profits accruing from the farming of taxes, from trading in landed property, or from money lending, as practised by the publicans. Doubtless, also, there were financial societies in the Roman world, as well as the bankers and money changers who carried on large financial operations. But the Romans were unacquainted with an elaborate credit organization, including the use of bills of exchange or transferable securities; and the Roman money changers and bankers cannot be compared with those modern bankers whose immense capital supplies industry and commerce and guides the functioning of economic life today.[1]

Even if we admit that capitalism had appeared in some

4

large commercial centers, the greater part of the Empire was not affected by this influence; for the rich classes lived principally on their rural estates and city life was of secondary importance. Hired workmen were hardly known, since labor was largely performed by slaves.

In the time of the Empire there were, to be sure, some organizations of artisans in the towns; but their membership (composed of freedmen) found great difficulty in competing against slave labor. Under a system of domestic and servile industry, both economic and social conditions were such that industrial capitalism could not develop. This characteristic alone serves to indicate how society in ancient times differed from that of today.[2] What we may call a *natural economy* characterized economic life; and, when the Empire crumbled, the institution of landed property alone survived.

II. THE FEUDAL RÉGIME AND THE PROGRESS OF INDIVIDUALISM

Beginning with the reign of Charlemagne—if not earlier in the period of the pre-Middle Ages—economic life was confined mainly to great rural manors. Town life fell away almost to nothing. Industry and commerce were greatly restricted; and, indeed, the renaissance of economic life in the time of Charlemagne is not a subject on which too many illusions should be encouraged. It is even possible that this period marked a setback, in the course of which, as a consequence of the Arab conquests, commercial activity (which had kept up, to some extent, since Roman times) was almost completely interrupted. Be that as it may, society came to be organized on a local basis, which permitted the manorial and feudal systems to develop, side by side. Under the restrictions imposed by this new social organization, new forms of economic activity could not get under way. None the less, the establishment of the feudal régime and the constitution of a military nobility did break down some of the more rigid regulations of the old system; and the resulting greater elasticity in economic and social life contributed, in turn, to the economic and social transformation which marks the triumph of individualism.

In the period of anarchy from which the feudal period emerged (the ninth to the eleventh centuries) the great lords sought to secure control over armed forces and to recruit a military following of knights (*milites*). The knight (*chevalier*, *miles*) need not have been possessed of fortune or landed estate, though such was frequently the case; but he must have been able to equip himself for mounted service and for combat on horseback. He was the "man" of the lord whom he served with his sword—his *vassus* or vassal; but, instead of receiving pay in money from this lord or *suzerain*, he obtained a holding of land, a fief.[3] Sometimes the knight was of humble birth (indeed he might even have been born a serf); but, whatever his origin, he was usually strong, brave, energetic, and fearless, a man thoroughly competent to follow his military chief on the field of battle.

At first, this practice of making concession of a fief implied only strictly personal relationships. But presently the hereditary character of the feudal relationship established itself; and the possession of a fief by the sons of nobles sufficed to determine their own noble condition. Entrance into the noble class was not closed to others, however, for commoners, possessors of fiefs, and those admitted to homage became nobles.

The disappearance of slavery, in the old sense of the word, and its replacement by serfdom, also tended to break down the barriers between social classes. In turn, serfdom tended to disappear gradually as the serfs secured exemptions, which relieved them from feudal duties, and especially those characterized by juridical obligations like *formariage*, and *mainmorte*.[4] Some of these exemptions, indeed, resulted from economic changes or conditions. Thus, beginning with the twelfth century, as clearings of land became more and more numerous, both lay and ecclesiastical lords invited the occupants, oftentimes runaway serfs, to cultivate them; and more liberal conditions of living were offered in order to hold their own serfs on the estates. Thus, serfdom, unlike slavery, did not constitute an unchanging condition of society.

Indeed, the various exemptions—which became very numerous in the thirteenth century—really broke down the barriers between the classes of feudal society. The rural population no longer formed a compact and uniform mass. On the contrary, there were many distinct ranks. Differences in economic condition led to many individuals' rising out of their previous position; and, among the serfs, there were some rich enough, or enterprising enough (and some who were favored by circumstances or a turn of good fortune) so that they attained places in the upper classes.

III. EARLY MANIFESTATIONS OF CAPITALISM IN FLORENCE

The town life of the Middle Ages furnished the favorable environment in which the first manifestations of capitalism appeared—at least in its purely commercial form; and it was principally in the city republics of Italy and in the Low Countries—two regions especially favored by economic conditions—that the first signs of capitalism appeared. Why were these two regions singled out as the first favored fields of capitalism? It was because the maritime commerce with the Orient, following the Crusades, endowed the Italian republics with a great store of capital. It was because the Low Countries served as the principal entrepôt in the commerce between the Orient and the North of Europe.[5]

The origin and development of capitalism in Italy are illustrated by the economic life of the great city of Florence. At

Florence, the trades were divided into three groups: the major arts, the middle arts, and the minor arts. The first group included merchants mainly: the sellers and finishers of foreign cloth (*arte di Calimala*); the manufacturers of cloth (*arte della lana*); and the merchants of novelties and silk goods *ettre de foire* and bill of exchange.[14] At first, accounts were necting the Occident and the Orient, early acquired a capitalistic character; and such was particularly the case in the trade carried on by the sellers and finishers of foreign cloth (the *arte di Calimala*). The masters in this trade made sales at wholesale; they had representation in the Levant and also frequented the European fairs, notably those of Brie and Champagne, where they bought French, Flemish and English cloths. Necessarily, they had a variety of subordinates in their employ, including not only agents and clerks, but also artisans and craftsmen, such as dyers, dressers, and shearers.

Since the merchants devised means for settling their accounts by bills of exchange, they presently began to carry on banking operations; and a group of money changers and bankers soon sprang up in Florence, specializing in this sort of business. These undertook a variety of commercial operations, including the exchange and shipment of precious metals and the supplying of funds for enterprises. They insured ships, received deposits, and made loans secured by pledges and mortgages.

The operations relating to public finance best served to enrich the bankers, however. Revenues accrued to the Holy See in all the countries of Christendom, including the tithes (Peter's Pence) in England; and the Church was everywhere receiving legacies and donations. Through their branches, the banking houses were in position to collect these revenues; and they were able to make advances of money to the pontifical court. Indeed, the Holy See utilized many banks in its financial transactions—houses in Siena, in Lucca, in Pistoia, and then in

Florence. In 1263 (under the pontificate of Urban IV) the Florentines managed to supplant the Sienese in this business.

The Florentine bankers also operated in the kingdom of Naples; and, in return, Charles of Anjou, who borrowed large sums from them, granted certain important commercial privileges and state monopolies. These were concerned with the exportation of wheat and wine, the iron mines, the salt taxes, etc. It is not surprising, therefore, that the owners of the Peruzzi bank received dividends of 40 per cent,—especially since the interest rate, currently 14 to 25 per cent, quite often rose to 45 or 50 per cent *per annum* when the loans were not contracted for on a monthly or weekly basis.

The importance of the Florentine banker was still further increased by the fall of the Templars in the fourteenth century; and, in the fifteenth century, the Medici (who had outdistanced the Spini, the Spigliati, the Bardi, the Pulci, and the Alfani) became so influential that they attained princely power. Indeed, the financial power of the Italian banker-capitalists became so great that they extended their operations over the whole of Western Christendom: to France, Spain, Portugal, and England. Sometimes they were attacked as usurers, and sometimes they received the same treatment as did the Cahorsins and the Jews.[6] But they proved to be necessary parts of the financial organization of the time; and everywhere noblemen and kings, prelates and towns, resorted to the Florentine and Lombard bankers. Two of these—Biche (*Biccio*) and Mouche (*Musciatto*)—became the "handy men" of Philip the Fair.

Thus, the Italians were the first to create a real system of financial capitalism;[7] and they were among the first to bring industry under the domination of capitalism, a development in the Low Countries, also. The cloth manufacturers (who constituted the *arte della lana* in Florence) after buying wool abroad, had it processed by numerous artisans in the city and country: weavers, fullers, dyers were completely dependent on them. This woolen industry, engaged in producing for the export market on a large scale, was thus an early example of that *domestic industry* which was later destined to play such a great part in the evolution of capitalism everywhere in Europe. When merchant trading (*arte di Calimala*) fell into decadence during the fourteenth century, it was supplanted by the manufacture of cloth (*arte della lana*). This in turn flourished until the middle of the fifteenth century. Then the silk industry (*arte della seta*) came to the forefront and held that position until close to the end of the sixteenth century, when France began to offer formidable competition. The maritime powers of the West had already achieved first place in commercial affairs in this period; and, thereafter, industrial life came to play a less important rôle in Italy.

IV. CAPITALISM IN THE LOW COUNTRIES

In the Low Countries, also, the first manifestation of capitalism (especially commercial capitalism) can be discerned as early as the Middle Ages. On the morrow of the Norman invasions,—and somewhat earlier than in most of the countries situated north of the Alps,—the Low Countries had begun to expand commercially. This expansion was favored by geographical conditions, for the Low Countries stand at the mouth of the Rhine Valley, one of the great natural highways between the Mediterranean region and the countries of the North.[8]

The great cities of the Low Countries (*portus* or *poorts*) like Bruges, Liège, Ghent, Brussels, Douai, Ypres, are founded at this time to serve as entrepôts of commerce. Such a trading city becomes "a permanent place for exchanging goods, and the center of a new economic activity." It is peopled principally by immigrants, many of them no doubt sons of serfs; and the majority earn their living as traders (*negociatores*). In this group, also, are adventurers, men of no very certain position in society but singularly energetic, prudent, and enterprising. Piracy first and then bold commercial operations enable members of this group to accumulate capital.

The merchants of the twelfth century are not specialists, however; they sell goods of all kinds, and the city is to them only a base of operations. They hasten from country to country and transport their merchandise from place to place. Since the roads are not safe, they form themselves into *guilds* and *hanse*, buying and selling in common, and sharing the profits "in proportion to their investments." In the course of their operations, credit instruments—such as the *lettre de foire* and the bill of exchange—are developed. Another result of the commercial expansion is an increase in the monetary stock. This, in turn, produces a rise of prices which has a serious reaction upon the situation in the countryside, since it stimulates the freeing of the peasants from their feudal obligations.

In the Low Countries, as in Italy, capitalism, although still maintaining its commercial form, presently spreads to industry. All the towns contain artisans—bakers, tailors, carpenters and the like—working for the local market. But there are also industries, such as the manufacture of cloth and brass, which are engaged in producing goods for sale in distant markets. In such trades, the workmen do not come into contact with the customers. Instead they are dominated by an exporting trader. In the cloth trade this is the draper, who often buys the wool himself, and sells the manufactured cloth. The actual making of the cloth is left to others; but, in any case, he takes charge of its finishing and sale. This draper is a capitalist; and the workmen, who are very numerous in the centers of the wool industry, are only wage earners.[9]

This form of economic organization (the domestic or "putting out" system) was really a new development, a development which foreshadowed modern large scale industry. Industries, which were capitalistic in their form of organization, developed only in a fairly limited number of towns, however, even in the Low Countries. The cities were scattered; and they were not, after all, very dense islets of population. Moreover, the system did not give rise to great concentrations of people; the population of Ypres, in the fifteenth century did not exceed 10,000 souls, and that of Ghent and Bruges was not over 40,000 to 50,000 people. Perhaps as many as 20,000 to 30,000 lived in Louvain, Brussels, and Liège.

The new form of industrial organization had an important consequence: the urban population was split into several clearly defined economic classes.[10] The cleavage between rich and poor became apparent; and out of the class of the newly enriched merchants and the *rentiers*, who possessed landed property and houses, a new group, the urban patriciate or aristocracy, was formed. Presently this latter group came into control of the governments of the cities. By the end of the Middle Ages, however, the expansion of capitalism in the towns and cities of the Low Countries was handicapped, as the common people revolted against the growing power of the urban patriciate. But this unsettlement did not prevent the emergence of an industrial organization which did not develop fully elsewhere until the eighteenth century.

The economic situation of the episcopal cities in the Low Countries was distinguished by a particular character, which Professor Pirenne has brought to light. Great export merchants were not found there; but, as the bishop was surrounded by a numerous court, a ready market was at hand for numerous furnishers, artisans, and merchants. Furthermore, the financial requirements of the ecclesiastic establishments—often quite considerable—led to the formation of a class of money changers and men of business. Their operations resulted in the creation of a true form of financial capitalism.

As early as the Middle Ages, it had been clear, moreover, that the Northern Low Countries were destined to become the seat of commercial capitalism. Commercial operations on a considerable scale developed early in Holland and Zeeland for the simple reason that nature did not furnish the inhabitants there everything necessary to economic life. Fishing, especially herring fishing, flourished very early, and considerable exportations of fish occurred. But Holland and Zeeland—which, to this day, are lands of pasturage and market gardens—did not produce the quantity of grain required for their own needs. To meet this situation, they drew first upon the rich plains of Picardy, and then upon the Baltic countries; and in due course the Low Countries came to constitute an entrepôt, to which several countries of Europe had recourse for their supplies.

Furthermore, the Northern Low Countries possessed but scanty supplies of wood for their shipbuilding operations; and they were without domestic supplies of metals. These deficiencies stimulated a powerful and growing trade in the fifteenth and sixteenth centuries, a trade which expanded marvelously in the seventeenth. The residents of the cities early played a leading rôle in this development; and it was at Middleburg, at Dordrecht, at Rotterdam, then at Amsterdam, that the economic life of the country was concentrated.[11]

V. FIRST SYMPTOMS IN FRANCE

The economic situation of the Italian republics and of the cities in the Low Countries appears to have been quite exceptional, however. We must not blind ourselves to the fact that elsewhere capitalism developed haltingly and only in very limited fashion. Commerce had not yet acquired a permanent character, at least on any considerable scale; instead, it was casual and intermittent. This latter condition was due to the inadequacy of the means of communication, the dangers of the road, and the absence of security, and to the small number of important urban centers.

Until the end of the Middle Ages, therefore, trading on any considerable scale was confined almost entirely to the fairs. Naturally, the most important fairs were located at strategic points, such as the intersections of the great land routes of communication. This influence accounts for the growth of the fairs of Champagne and Lyons. Sometimes also, as in the case of the Flemish fairs, these important gatherings of traders were held near the great centers of production. The decline of the fairs followed improvement in the regular transportation service and in the roads, the establishment of an effective police, and the increase of large urban centers. Gradually, the fairs gave place to *bourses;* and the growth of the latter coincided with the development of permanent commercial relations.

In the Middle Ages the economic development of the regions which made up the French kingdom was less advanced than that of the Italian cities and the Low Countries. Industry and trade were almost entirely in the hands of artisans and merchants, who possessed only very limited resources and were not capitalists in any sense. Gradually, however, a group of wholesale merchants emerged from the men of a trade; and members of this group, notably the mercers, began to accumulate capital. A curious statute of the fifteenth century concerning the prerogative of the "king of mercers" indicates the variety of goods which the mercers sold and the economic control which they exercised over a number of trades. The fact that a royal ordinance of 1413 exempts the mercers from the inspection of the trade examiners (*jurés des métiers*) is not astonishing, therefore.

On the other hand, maritime commerce on a large scale—one of the great sources of capitalism—had really appeared only in regions not yet incorporated into the French kingdom,

Provence for example. Following the Crusades, Provence had maintained an active trade with a number of ports in the Levant in the twelfth and thirteenth centuries; and Bordeaux maintained close commercial relations with England, the country which controlled Guienne until the middle of the fifteenth century. In 1213, the shipowners of Bayonne formed a society for mutual assistance and profit sharing; and, as early as the thirteenth century, there were fairly numerous examples of companies with limited liability at Marseilles. In the kingdom proper, on the other hand, few important merchant guilds, as they were called in the Low Countries, seem to have developed, though "the merchants frequenting the river Loire" seem to have formed such an organization.

Furthermore, it must be remembered that the economic expansion of the kingdom of France was hindered, indeed paralyzed, by the ravages of the terrible Hundred Years' War. It is only after this war—that is, in the second half of the fifteenth century—that commercial relations developed anew (as shown by the creation of numerous fairs) or that the accumulation of "mobile" wealth really went on.

Louis XI sought to foster the development of commerce to a greater extent than had his predecessors, and he endeavored to introduce luxury industries into France during his reign (1461–1483). Here he was following a mercantilist conception, because he considered that the purchase of precious cloth stuffs from abroad diminished the monetary stock of the kingdom. Such was the essential reason for his attempt to establish the silk industry, first at Lyons, where it failed because of opposition on the part of the inhabitants, and then at Tours, where it prospered during his reign. Thus manufacturing on a large scale (*la grande industrie*)—in France long destined to produce only luxury objects—owed its existence to the initiative and encouragement of the state. It is also significant that Louis XI, anticipating the efforts of Colbert two centuries later, wished to create a large commercial company with special privileges to trade with the East, the *Compagnie du Levant*. Indeed, the development of commercial capitalism in France, like the creation of large scale industrial operations, was destined to be largely the result of special efforts on the part of the government.

VI. CAPITALISM IN ENGLAND

During the greater part of the Middle Ages, and even in the thirteenth and fourteenth centuries, England appears to have been an exclusively agricultural country. Manufacturing was confined to the petty city trades. In spite of its island position, the maritime power of England was unimportant and its commerce was almost entirely in the hands of foreigners. Not until the fourteenth century did the Staplers begin to devote themselves to international commerce, principally the export trade in English wool.

By the end of the Middle Ages, however, the first signs of commercial capitalism appear in England. The wealth of certain urban trades—notably the mercers, grocers, and drapers—soon causes these merchant trades to stand out from the rest. Commercial capitalism gains greater strength as the woolen or cloth industry develops during the fifteenth century; and the arrival of Flemish and Brabantine refugees in England contributes to the success of this new industry.[12] A new class of cloth merchants, the drapers, appears, and England begins to export the cloth she is manufacturing. The progress of the woolen industry contributes in marked degree to the breaking down of the manorial system and gives birth to the practice of enclosure, which in time eliminates the small peasant holdings.

During the course of the fifteenth and sixteenth centuries, the textile industry pretty generally abandons the towns for the country, and a system of *rural and domestic industry* is created. So far as the origin of English capitalism is concerned, this is a most important step. In this system of industry (the domestic or "putting out" system), commercial capitalism, already greatly strengthened by the export trade in cloth, extends its activities to exercise control over manufacturing operations. In truth, commercial capitalism comes to "control" industry, to use a modern expression. Under this system of business organization, as Sir William Ashley has said so well, the clothier (textile manufacturer) bought the wool, had it woven, fulled, and dyed; he paid the artisans at each stage of the manufacture and he sold the manufactured merchandise to the drapers. Thus, he played the part of a capitalist in relation to the artisans (although the capital of most of these merchant-manufacturers was still inconsiderable); and, at the same time, he was economically dependent on the export market. Interruption of trade abroad necessarily meant a suspension of operations by manufacturers and a period of unemployment for the artisans in their employ. Indeed, such were the consequences when the rupture of diplomatic relations between England and the Emperor in 1527 deprived the merchants of a foreign market for their cloth.

The second emigration of the Flemish to England, following the religious persecutions in the latter half of the sixteenth century, still further accentuated the economic evolution already under way; and at this time Norwich became an important center for the cloth industry. Moreover, as appears later on, the system of *rural and domestic industry* grew up everywhere in Europe, though more tardily, it seems, than in England.

During this phase of the economic evolution, the Merchant Adventurers, those gallant precursors of the great maritime expansion of England, seized upon their opportunity. Instead of contenting themselves with relatively limited markets like the Staplers, the Merchant Adventurers looked far afield. Here was a striking example of the reciprocal influences which commercial activity and industrial activity exercised upon each other!

Even in Spain, a country which was outside the great commercial routes and where the economic life was not very active, some manifestations of incipient capitalism appeared as early as the Middle Ages. This was notably the case in Seville, where the development of a new economic organization was facilitated mainly by the activities of the Genoese and the Jews.[13]

VII. FINANCIAL CAPITALISM AND ITS CHARACTER

Financial capitalism also developed during the Middle Ages, mainly as an outgrowth of commercial capitalism, for most of those who transacted financial business had been engaged previously in the merchandise trade as drapers, grocers, or mercers. In Italy, the wholesale merchants of the *arte di Calimala* were of this class, as were the financiers of Arras in the Low Countries, notably the Crespin family. Even the Lombards, whose money-lending establishments (*tables de prêt*) were so numerous in the Low Countries, did not confine their operations solely to financial affairs.

The accumulation of considerable capitals in the hands of the moneyed merchants was furthered by the growing practice of borrowing on the part of princes, cities, and ecclesiastical establishments, not to mention mere lords and members of the middle class (*bourgeois*). Such debts bore high rates of interest—seldom less than 20 or 25 per cent, and sometimes as much as 50 or 60 per cent. The class of financiers was also recruited from the financial functionaries of the princes, both secular and ecclesiastical. Many of these functionaries were of Italian origin, a fact readily understood since the Italians had a great grasp of the technical aspects of financial affairs.

Another great stimulus toward creating a system of financial capitalism was the variety of specie which circulated and the consequent necessity for creating means of changing and transferring money, even in a small area. Everywhere, therefore, a great number of money changers appeared, particularly in places where international commerce was carried on; and a system for money changing was nowhere more important than in the great fairs of Champagne, where merchants congregated from all over Europe. It was at these fairs (around the thirteenth century) that the practice developed of using the *lettre de foire* and bill of exchange.[14] At first, accounts were settled in cash; but subsequently a credit system developed, and it was but a short step to devise means for extinguishing debts evidenced by bills of exchange. This was done by the device of compensation, *i. e.*, the parties to the bills were exchanged. This operation, called *scontration*, while first developed at the Lyons fairs, was further perfected at the Spanish fairs and the fairs at Genoa. Thus it was at the fairs (as Paul Huvelin says very correctly) that merchandise and money ceased to be objects of consumption and became capital. Moreover, although those engaged in financial operations did not constitute a wholly independent group during the Middle Ages, the importance of the position they were destined to occupy in economic life does begin to loom up.

Maritime commerce played a rôle analogous to that of the fairs. As early as the thirteenth century, foreign exchange operations were carried on at Bruges, though on a smaller scale than at the fairs of Champagne; but it was Antwerp which was destined to become the great center of international trade and exchange at the end of the fifteenth century and in the sixteenth. As someone has well said, this city (and especially the Antwerp *Bourse*) came to constitute a permanent fair.

It has been asserted that, in the Low Countries at least, the system of public borrowing was not favorable to the development of a financial group in the community. The contrary seems to have been the case in most countries; for, beginning with the Middle Ages, the progress of the princely states contributed in high degree to the development of financial capitalism. Princes were forced to turn to the men of wealth for funds to finance their administrative operations, their political undertakings, and above all their wars. Upon occasion (and such occasions often presented themselves) these men of wealth would agree to advance considerable sums; and in return the princes conceded monopoly privileges, like those of the *tables de prêt*, which conferred the right to lend money against pledges—the original lombard-houses or pawnshops. Without any doubt, as Professor Sombart shows, fairly close relations can be traced between the evolution of the state and that of capitalism. But while this relationship stands out even more clearly in the following centuries, it is certainly only one of the sources of capitalism.

The mechanism of the exchanges, as well as the borrowings of the princely states, necessarily involved lending at interest; and this practice (at least when it did not represent the profit of a limited company or take the form of ground rent) was one condemned by the Church. But, lending at interest is, if not the principal source, at least the essential manifestation of capitalism; and it was certain, therefore, that the force of circumstances would bring recognition of the practice in the legislation of the various states.

Commercial societies were another development of Italy during the Middle Ages. These were the forerunners of the corporation which has played such a great part in the genesis and evolution of modern capitalism. These commercial societies took two forms: (1) the *société en commandite* (limited joint stock company), which made possible the undertaking of commercial operations on a larger scale; and (2) the *société en nom collectif* (company under a collective name), which perhaps derived its name from the common interests of a family. Joint stock companies, as we know them, did not really develop until the seventeenth century.

It was likewise in Italy, during the Middle Ages, that sea loans and maritime insurance, which are so closely allied with the history of capitalism, grew up.[15] By the end of the Middle Ages, the practice of insurance had spread to the other maritime countries of Europe. The great Portuguese merchants appear to have contributed greatly to this progress, as in all the elaboration of commercial law, though, unfortunately, works on this subject are few. "Private" insurance alone existed at first; for insurance companies did not originate until the seventeenth century when the great advantages arising from a division of the risks fostered their formation.

VIII. THE POWERFUL FINANCIERS OF THE MIDDLE AGES

Considerable is now known concerning the financial interests and banking houses of the Middle Ages. Some of these confined their operations pretty much to one city or one country, and the financiers of Arras (in particular, the Crespins and Loucharts), whom Georges Bigwood has recently described to us, were of this class. Their wealth was accumulated, it appears, through both commercial operations and the income from their properties, including ground rents. In the thirteenth century and at the beginning of the fourteenth, they had sufficient capital at their disposal to make very considerable loans to princes, like the Count of Saint-Pol and the Count of Artois, to secular and ecclesiastical lords, and to cities in the Low Countries, such as Bruges. They had their seat in the city of Arras, and maintained no representatives outside. They operated without international connections and went to the fairs to carry on their trade.

William of Duvenvoorde (1290–1353), counselor of Count William of Holland, was quite a different sort of person. His wealth was accumulated mainly from financial transactions: exchange operations, speculation in ground rents, the advancing of sums to individuals and particularly to princes, and lending upon the security of lucrative mortgages. So great was his wealth that he had an annual income of 70,000 *livres*. In 1404, his grandniece married Englebert of Nassau; and thus it is to a *nouveau-riche* of the fourteenth century that the house of Orange-Nassau owes its pecuniary fortune, and consequently its political fortune.

The most important financial organizations developed during the Middle Ages were, however, those with connections in various countries. Such, for example, were the powerful Italian banks, which had branches in numerous countries, and the money changers and Lombards who were found throughout the Christian world. Such also were the members of the Hanseatic League, with their important establishments in many of the principal cities throughout northwest Europe.

The Jews also occupied an international position of economic power. Scattered about everywhere though they were, they were held together by the ties of that religion which had brought both humiliation and persecution upon them. Therefore, they found themselves particularly well placed for undertaking important commercial and financial operations. It has been believed that the Jews confined their early business activities solely to financial transactions; but the contrary seems to have been the case: until the thirteenth century, the Jews were engaged primarily in the merchandise trade rather than in financial affairs.[16]

Finally, the Church itself appears as an international financial power during the Middle Ages. The bishops, chapters, and abbeys possessed great landed properties; and the necessity of selling their produce, grain, and wool led them to carry on trade for their own account. Subsequently they undertook to trade for the account of others, despite the prohibitions of church councils, which became more frequent with the constant violations of the rulings forbidding such operations.

Presently, indeed, the church authorities began to carry on a traffic in funds. The monasteries became veritable credit establishments,[17] and the great military orders, with their commanderies in many countries, which provided every facility for carrying on lucrative exchange dealings, had a large interest in financial affairs. Thus, the Teutonic Order gave quite as much attention to commercial and financial transactions as to Christianizing the Slavs, who were still heathen; and the Templars, who held considerable deposits of precious metals and money, lent large sums to nobles, princes, and kings, whose treasurers they really became. They carried on various banking operations, and accumulated so much wealth that they tempted the cupidity of Philip the Fair, a sovereign who was always short of money. The scandalous trial and destruction of their order was due to this circumstance.[18]

The foregoing sketch suffices to show how various were the sources of capitalism in the Middle Ages. Clearly Professor Sombart's contention that capitalism developed mainly out of the operation of the properties of the lords, and from the increase of the urban properties and ground rents held by the urban patriciate is too narrow.[19] Doubtless these sources contributed to the growth of capitalism; but they were much less fertile sources than the great international trade in goods or the financial operations which grew out of that trade. International relations, though still exceptional in the Middle Ages, had already begun to play an important rôle in the economic life of the time; and whoever wishes to understand the accumulation of capital will find such relations the most considerable single factor to be taken into account.

One final remark: it was chiefly financial operations which gave rise to the class of the newly rich. But new figures arose in each generation, as Professor Pirenne has shown so well. The descendants of those who had accumulated great fortunes did not wait long before abandoning the world of business. They bought manors or urban properties, acquired sources of income such as ground rents and the debts of princes and cities, and penetrated the ranks of the landed aristocracy or the urban patriciate. In a word, they renounced economic activity, and stood only as representatives of the past. The newcomers took up the torch and in their turn created new forms of activity which furthered the evolution of modern capitalism.

IX. NON-EXISTENCE OF INDUSTRIAL CAPITALISM

During the Middle Ages, capitalism appeared only in its purely commercial form, and industrial capitalism, in the modern sense of the word, did not exist in any shape. The artisans, especially those engaged in the trades providing food, clothing, building construction and furniture, themselves provided the means of production. But that these means of production were generally very meagre is shown, for example, by the register of the poll tax (*taille*) in Paris in 1292, and by the excise taxes of Basel in the fifteenth century. The craftsman worked alone or with one or two companions, and he produced not for distant markets, but for local consumers to whom he sold his products directly. Sometimes he worked up raw materials furnished by the clients.

The corporate régime (the organization of trade guilds), as it existed everywhere in the Middle Ages, tended to keep the craftsmen in a fairly humble situation, by preventing competition, by limiting the number of apprentices, and by ensuring to each master the few hands he absolutely needed.

In the great majority of the towns, the craft guilds were able to maintain the régime of small industries, not only during the Middle Ages, but well into modern times. Only in the merchant guilds did distinctions between the masters appear; and it was in these guilds, for the most part, that the accumulation of capital took place. This is a very significant fact.

X. CONCLUSION

The foregoing discussion leads to the conclusion that, contrary to the frequent contention, capitalism was not unknown in the Middle Ages. During that period, the first manifestations of capitalism appeared in those regions where international commerce had developed—notably in Italy and the Low Countries. In fact, the urban economy was not entirely closed to outside influences (as some have often declared) and several important currents of trade were well established. Moreover, the Crusaders opened the East and gave an opportunity to the Italian traders—a condition which promoted the accumulation of capital and thus furthered the early economic development of the Italian republics. The resulting system of capitalism was concerned mainly with commercial affairs and did not take hold of industry except in some towns of Italy and the Low Countries. Meanwhile, however, financial capitalism had already appeared. It developed mainly, during the Middle Ages, as an outgrowth of commercial capitalism; but the financial needs of the kings, princes, and cities also contributed toward building up the large fortunes of some of the capitalists—the financiers of Arras, for example, and William of Duvenvoorde. Great financial powers also appeared, such as the Italian banks, the Hanseatic merchants, the Jews, and the religious orders, which, by virtue of their international character, possessed facilities for the convenient transfer of securities. They were in position also to carry on the banking operations essential to those engaged in large scale commercial transactions, and to the kings and princes whose political activities necessitated important financial transactions. These first manifestations of capitalism did not play more than a secondary rôle in the Europe of the Middle Ages, however; and even in the towns, the system of small scale operations in the hands of craftsmen was the basis of the whole manufacturing organization. Landed property, then dominated by the manorial system, held first place in the economic life of England and Germany, as well as in that of France.

CHAPTER III

THE BEGINNING OF MODERN TIMES

I. THE GENESIS OF CAPITALISM: SOMBART'S THEORY

OBVIOUSLY a capitalistic society could develop only with the accumulation of capital. At the outset, therefore, the question presents itself: what were the sources of this accumulation at the dawn of modern times? According to Werner Sombart, commerce, as carried on in the Middle Ages, was incapable of producing a store of capital; and he has collected certain facts indicating the smallness of commercial profits in those days. Yet these data, though they appear fairly impressive, are not numerous enough to be entirely convincing. Moreover, local commerce should be distinguished carefully from the intercity or international commerce, which was steadily developing in the last centuries of the Middle Ages. The urban economy was never so closed (*geschlossen*) as Bücher imagines;[1] and the wool and cloth trade of Italy and the Low Countries really appears to have been the original source, or at least one of the sources, of the great fortunes built up in these countries by a relatively early date.

The further fact should also be taken into consideration that business was far from being truly specialized in organization. Thus, the merchandise trade and the money trade were often in the same hands; and the goldsmiths often lent money, thus acting as bankers. Yet it is true (and this is what seems really sound in Sombart's theory) that capital was often accumulated by persons who collected taxes and

excises for the account of kings or the Holy See or even the
revenues of the great land owners, both ecclesiastic and secular. And it should also be admitted, as he urges, that lending money at interest, as practised by the Lombards and the
Jews, may be considered one of the sources of capitalism.

The exploitation of mineral resources likewise played a
fairly important rôle in this respect. This is shown in the
experience of the Fuggers. Professor Jakob Strieder, basing
his opinion on very numerous documents, has shown that, as
early as the fifteenth century, these exploitations had led to
the formation of the *Aktiengesellschaften*—something like
the present day corporations.[2] Many such were in the hands
of rich members of the middle class (*bourgeois*) in Southern
Germany. Doubtless, also, the increment in the value of
landed property, as cities increased in population and wealth,
must be taken into account.[3] This unearned increment was
often enormous in amount and accrued mainly to the patriciate of the towns. This group often allied itself with the rural
nobility and succeeded in mingling with it. But the urban
patriciate, which had gained its wealth and power through
commerce, seems to have played a less active part, in this early
expansion of capitalism, than that played by the "new men."
It was the class of the newly rich, as Professor Pirenne has
well said, who here played the most active part.

II. THE GREAT FINANCIAL POWERS OF ITALY AND GERMANY. THE *BOURSES* OR EXCHANGES

Consideration of the great financial powers, which had
sprung up by the end of the Middle Ages, is necessary for an
understanding of the origin of financial capitalism. Their development, as Richard Ehrenberg shows, was chiefly the result of public borrowing, made necessary by the formation of
the great states, princely or monarchical. At this time the
interest rate was often over 50 per cent. These states had

expanded their needs for funds, and their requirements to meet military, diplomatic, and financial expenses grew steadily. Public finance became a much more important branch of business.

This condition explains the financial activity of the Italians (Florentines, Genoese, natives of Lucca) in England, in the Low Countries, and in France, and the importance of the *marans* (converted Portuguese Jews) at Antwerp. In Germany there were the Fuggers of Augsburg, a family which, starting as merchants, presently took over copper and silver mines. Next the Fuggers became bankers and presently they were the recognized bankers of the Hapsburgs, and played an important part in the election of Charles V. Other Augsburg and Nuremberg houses—such as the family of Tuchers and the Imhofs—were great financial powers in the first half of the sixteenth century; and German bankers also occupied a considerable place in financial circles abroad. At Lyons, for example, there was "the good Kleberg," who was for years the most important personage of that city. The financial group in the community was also greatly increased by the commercial societies, syndicates, and monopolies.

A significant fact is that the large fairs, which had played such an important part when large scale commerce still had a solely periodic character, gradually lost their former importance, as "sedentary" and urban commerce developed. As early as the sixteenth century, *bourses* or exchange places were being formed. Certain of these, like the *bourses* of Antwerp and Lyons, were destined to become of world-wide importance.

In the fairs, financial transactions had originated only as a consequence of commercial transactions; but at the *bourses* or exchange places, the actual goods were no longer brought to the market place. The trading was done only in terms of securities which represented goods. The *bourse* at Lyons, as a matter of fact, owed its importance rather to finance than to

commerce, and its development was in part the work of the
kings of France. It became the favored place for negotiating
public loans, and the bankers, for the most part natives of
Italy or Southern Germany, congregated there. In the end,
Lyons lost its banking importance, and was transformed into
a great industrial city.

In the sixteenth century, as Richard Ehrenberg shows, the
emphasis shifted from the fairs to the *bourses*, both in the
merchandise trade and in financial matters. At the fairs,
transactions could take place only on occasion; in the *bourses*,
on the contrary, the trade in merchandise and securities might
be carried on every day of the year. The development of
the *bourse*, therefore, contributed greatly to the concentration
of commercial and financial operations. The *bourse* was open
"to the merchants of all nations," as says the inscription on
the pediment of the Antwerp *Bourse*, the establishment of
which, in 1531, was an event of great significance in the
history of capitalism.[4]

Because of the *bourses*, political events and opinion came
to have a great deal of influence upon business. This explains
the origin of the gazettes, which furnished the traders with
the news they required. The *bourse* also reacted on the credit
position of individuals—for it was very important for a
business man to have a good name on 'change, a *buona ditta*,
as the Italian expression has it. The *bourse* was also important for public credit. Finally, there was nothing more
important for the life of a commercial center than the "prices
current" for goods; and the rate of interest as established
on the exchange took into account both the vicissitudes of the
public credit and events at home and abroad.

III. SPECULATION IN CAPITAL

In the sixteenth century also—and as early as the first
half of that century—methods were devised for carrying on

speculative operations in capital. These consisted both of the premium trade (*marché à prime*)—a sort of bet on prices and exchange rates, which could be used as insurance against excessive fluctuations in exchange—and, especially, of arbitrage operations. The latter depended on the difference of prices and exchange rates in different places: a kind of speculation which might make possible a gain as high as 5 per cent in a period of 15 or 20 days. Arbitrage, which had been carried on in the Middle Ages by the Italians, presupposes a great deal of perspicacity and mastery of a real and difficult science; it calls also for an ability to appraise a wide variety of diverse conditions and considerations.

Another important development came in the field of maritime insurance. While insurance had been invented in Italy, and had spread to Portugal, its progress was very great during the sixteenth century, especially at Antwerp. The amount of the premiums became better defined and participation in insurance speculation became more general. In 1564, this business afforded an affluent living to 600 persons. Some of the brokers were none too honest, and frequently all sorts of frauds, such as might inure to the profit of the insurers or the insured, were promoted. It was not until 1559 that the sovereign attempted to regulate the business. No insurance companies yet existed, though often a great number of individuals acted as insurers of a single vessel. At Antwerp the practice also grew up of insuring lives, or rather journeys, without the knowledge of the insured. This situation led to bad frauds and even to crimes.

The close relationship between insurance and speculation is clear enough, because insurance, even when carried on honestly, always implies assumption of a risk, at least by the insurer. But this risk is one which is destined to become less as the institution becomes better established. A society in which speculation has developed is also likely to be one characterized by a taste for gambling in all its forms. One result of this was the organization of lotteries, like the great lottery of 1565–1567, which proved profitable mainly to Margaret of Parma, natural daughter of Charles V, the Regent of the Low Countries, and to its organizers. The practice of betting also grew up: at Antwerp they even bet on the sex of children before birth (a great opportunity for fraud), or on the running time of a horse over a certain course, or on the date of an historic event. In the feverish atmosphere of Antwerp in the sixteenth century a whole world of promoters of more or less chimerical projects appeared—purveyors of advice, men with many irons in the fire, and also inventors and engineers. A good number of these were plain swindlers, but there are also some really interesting figures, such as Gaspard Ducci and Leonardo di Benavento.

The great consequence of the progress of speculation was the mobilization of capital, and the transaction of business in the documents which represented certain goods (or were supposed to represent them) rather than in the actual merchandise. Even landed property began to be so "mobilized," thanks to the development of the mortgage.

IV. FINANCIAL CRISES AND THE PROGRESS OF PUBLIC CREDIT

Another new phenomenon of the century was the international financial crisis which grew out of the development of public credit.

In France, the Cardinal de Tournon attempted to create an institution based on the public credit. Acting in the interest of the King, he caused all the deposits of the Lyonnaise banks to be centralized, promising a return of 10 per cent at least. Then, again at Lyons, in 1554, a veritable public loan (the *grand parti*) was floated; and all sorts of persons, including the humblest, were approached on this occasion. Even servants put their savings into the *grand parti*. There was a regular frenzy of speculation, though foreigners did not prove in the least eager to participate. Subscribers received bonds or obligations; but a collapse soon followed and the paper depreciated, first by 15 per cent, then, in 1559, by 30 and even 50 per cent. Contemporaneously, the Spanish state suffered from a similar crisis. These bankruptcies had serious effects on all the money dealers: twenty million ducats ($50,000,000), if not dissipated, were at least seriously involved; and public credit was severely injured. The Wars of Religion brought on another grave crisis. Moreover, they led to the downfall of the *bourses* at Antwerp and Lyons, two cities which very largely went over to the side of the Reformation.

Another and new bankruptcy of the Spanish state, occurring in 1575, naturally precipitated a very serious crisis. It shattered the prosperity of the Spanish fairs (of Medina del Campo and of Villalon, for example) where trading had taken place on a large scale and where the Fuggers and the Genoese bankers had played an important rôle. This bankruptcy affected Nicolo Grimaldi, certain Spanish financiers like Espinosa, the capitalists of Seville and Burgos, as well as many private individuals.

It is readily seen how the princes, whose needs for money constantly increased, should have served the cause of capitalism. So far as the Low Countries are concerned, this has been shown very clearly by Professor Pirenne. The artisans of the towns fought the monarchical régime vigorously only because it menaced town exclusivism, to which the triumph of capitalism would be disastrous. Such was the real meaning of the revolt of Ghent in 1477 and the troubles which followed it. Philip the Fair favored Antwerp which represented the new spirit, to the detriment of Bruges; and again, around 1500, he sacrificed the cloth industry of Flanders and

Brabant to the interests of Antwerp which was carrying on a lucrative business in finishing English cloth.

Thus, it appears impossible to deny the relationship between the development of monarchies, of great states, and the progress of capitalism. The importance of the great financial houses, the Fuggers and those who imitated them, was singularly increased by the borrowings of princes and the requirements of the public credit.

V. THE DEVELOPMENT OF BANKS

The progress of banking is another characteristic of the epoch. Such institutions were founded principally by Italians, who had gained considerable experience in banking enterprises by the Middle Ages, and also by Germans. At Lyons, for example, numerous banks were created by individuals of both nationalities;[5] and their existence made that city a great international center for money dealings. These banks accepted deposits from men of all classes, nobles as well as merchants; and some bankers undertook vast speculations with the money deposited with them. One such speculator was Ambrose Hoechstetter, who sought to corner the mercury market, and who ended by ruining both himself and his silent partners.

The development of banks introduced new customs. This is forcibly shown by Ludovico Guiccardini, who has left us a vivid description of Antwerp in the sixteenth century:

"Formerly, the nobles who had available funds invested them in lands, a sort of investment which gave work to many people and furnished the country's needs. The merchants employed their capital in their regular trade, in a manner to equalize famine and superabundance among the different countries; they utilized countless men and augmented the revenues of the princes and the towns. Today, on the contrary, a part of the nobility and the merchants (the first through the intermediary of the second, and the others openly), in order to avoid the pains and perils of regular professional activity, devote all their disposable capital to the money trade, which attracts them by its high and certain gains."

1476037

VI. COMMERCIAL CAPITALISM AS THE SOURCE OF FINANCIAL CAPITALISM

Yet however great the influence of the money trade and speculation upon the genesis of capitalism, they clearly did not constitute its most fruitful source. By themselves, they could not have founded a solid and durable economic power. This is well shown by Ehrenberg when he compares the fairs of Genoa with those of Frankfort.

The fairs of Genoa acquired great importance after the downfall of Antwerp, and continued to flourish for half a century. Their outstanding characteristic was that no trading in merchandise took place; the Genoa fairs were the seat of financial transactions. Such trading was particularly active, however, since there was opportunity to effect exchange operations with the principal commercial centers of Europe. The Spanish Crown often did business at the Genoa fairs in order to meet its financial requirements. Moreover, since there was opportunity for carrying on all sorts of speculative transactions, the fairs favored the concentration of very considerable capitals. On the other hand, the fact that these fairs did not constitute permanent commercial centers meant that they harked back to the past rather than announced the future. They were the last brilliant flash of the economic life of the Middle Ages.

On the other hand, the downfall of Antwerp greatly increased the power of Frankfort, which had attained the most important place in Western Germany by the end of the Middle Ages. The fairs held there were not of a purely financial character, however; some very active trading in merchandise and actual transfers of goods took place. The growth in importance of the Frankfort fair was slower than that of the Genoese fair; but, on the other hand, the former became better established and had a more lasting success. Even during the Thirty Years' War, the fair was held; and Frankfort continued to play a great part as late as the eighteenth century, even though coming to depend more and more upon Amsterdam. The proof of this prosperity is that the interest rate was never very high there; it rarely exceeded 5 or 6 per cent and went even lower.

A glance at England in the sixteenth century shows that financial capitalism was coming to life there. This change was singularly favored by the development of industry and the progress of commercial capitalism. The output of the cloth industry more than doubled in value during the second half of the century; and this expansion created a need for capital, a need met by the merchants engaged in the export trade. Exploitation of the mining resources, which was steadily progressing, also called for capital.

Development of the export trade also brought the foreign exchange problem into a position of greater importance. London doubtless did not possess the financial organization of Antwerp or Lyons; but, thanks to its commerce, London found itself possessing direct relations with the great foreign markets, especially with Antwerp, Hamburg, Lyons, and Rouen.

Moreover, since the value of money often differed quite considerably from place to place, operations in foreign exchange produced great profits and gave rise to active speculation. Such operations should not be confused with the mere changing of money, because two elements enter into the exchange operations: the interest rate and the daily variation of the exchange rates themselves.

stous More Pinxit.   I.B. Michel Sculpsit.

Sir **THOMAS** **GRESHAM**.

In the Common Parlour at Houghton
Size of the Picture   2.1 by 2.9 3/4 high
Published May 1.st 1779 by John Boydell Engraver in Cheapside London.

That many English merchants, grown rich through the cloth business, found it more advantageous to carry on speculation on the exchanges than to continue their old trade is shown by the great merchant, Sir Thomas Gresham, who wrote in the time of Henry VIII. These English merchants traded mainly on the Antwerp *bourse*, and their operations often brought in as much as 16 per cent without involving them in great risks. This fact alone would explain the development of what has been called "dry exchange," the business of speculation, which the Church condemned as usurious. The situation in England is a striking example of the close connections which obtained between commercial transactions and banking operations during the sixteenth century.

VII. LENDING AT INTEREST: THE CHURCH AND THE NEW PRACTICES

In England, as in all Western Europe, very important questions arose presently concerning loans at interest (usury) and the exchange value of money.

The doctrine of the canon law (which condemned lending at interest) reigned supreme during the Middle Ages. But even during this epoch—when, as in antiquity, the investment of money was conceived of as a form of usury—the legitimacy of a loan came to be recognized, provided it had to do with a limited joint stock company. Participation in such an enterprise was held to imply the assumption of risks and indemnification.

The Church therefore sought to distinguish between sterile loans and productive loans. In England, Cardinal Morton, Chancellor in the time of Henry VII, declared to Parliament: "His Grace (the King) prays you to take into consideration matters of trade, as also the manufactures of the kingdom, and to restrain the bastard and barren employment of moneys in usury and unlawful exchanges; that they may be, as their natural use is, turned upon commerce and lawful and royal trading." [6]

Furthermore, it should be remembered, the Church recognized as legitimate the income-yielding lease (*bail à rente*) which is, in fact, merely a sort of disguised loan. Sir William Ashley has forcefully remarked that, as commercial relations were extended, money came more and more to assume the character of capital; and, as Mr. Tawney says, "doctrines designed to protect the peasant or craftsman against the pawnbroker were not equally applicable to the clothiers, mine owners, and iron-masters, who were quite capable of protecting themselves." [7]

The scholastic doctrine persisted, however; and, for such traders and men of business as remained true to the Catholic faith, the problems of conscience proved singularly embarrassing. This condition explains the curious address which Jean-Baptiste, the Franciscan, presented to the University of Paris at the request of the Spanish merchants of Antwerp whose confessor he was. The curious document which contained the answer to this address has come down to our time.[8] It shows clearly that the Catholic theologians had not renounced any of their traditional ideas. They rejected the "interest on exchange" as illicit and usurious; they denounced every speculative element in commerce and approved only the repayment of expenses incurred by a lender; and they absolutely condemned return exchange (*change de retour*) and dry exchange (*change sec*), in a word, all speculation on exchange and securities.[9] But it is quite evident that business practices could not be governed by these rigid rules. The Spanish sovereigns Charles V and Philip II—good Catholics though they were—borrowed heavily, and they found it necessary to recognize the legitimacy of interest, provided it was relatively moderate, say not to exceed 12 per cent.

Public authority in England, at the time of the Tudors, was also very much embarrassed by the questions raised by loans at interest and the exchanges. To hold to the old conception of the Church, and to continue to consider a loan as "the accursed sin" was seen to be impossible; and so it was argued that what was reprehensible was not the payment of a reasonable and legitimate sum for the money lent, but only the exactions to which a loan at interest might give rise. In 1545 a royal act authorized interest at 10 per cent. This was abrogated in 1552, to be sure; but, as early as 1571, it was again made operative. Thus the cause of lending at interest was won in England, despite the resistance of the Anglican Church, or the opposition of many writers, like Thomas Wilson whose *Discourse upon Usury* (1572) made no concessions to the new ideas. And this Thomas Wilson, as Mr. Tawney remarks, was not a theologian at all, but a public official of high position, a cultured magistrate, well informed and quite "up to date" on economic questions.

VIII. THE INFLUENCE OF CALVINISM

It must be recognized that the capitalistic attitude of mind had already manifested itself (as early as the Middle Ages) in the Italian towns, which were wholly Catholic. Can it be said therefore that the Calvinistic Reforms, and particularly Puritanism, contributed to the development of capitalism by creating a capitalistic mentality, as Max Weber and Ernst Troeltsch assert? Without question, the doctrine of Calvin, in so far as it concerns lending at interest, ran counter to the doctrine of the Catholic Church. This was because Calvin did not believe in barriers between the spiritual and the temporal: he considered work and the serious exercise of a profession as praiseworthy, and therefore accepted the acquisition of riches as legitimate. Lending money at interest did not appear to him

any more to be condemned than the making of a commercial
profit. From this point of view, his doctrine approached the
Jewish conception, and we shall later have occasion to examine the consequences of this. Moreover, the simplicity of life
of the Puritans contributed to the accumulation of wealth,
and their *moral* virtues were often transformed into *economic*
virtues. But Puritanism also gave birth to ultra-democratic
doctrines in the England of the seventeenth century. The
truth seems to be, therefore, that the individualism character-
izing the Calvinistic Reform fitted well with the individualism which characterized the economic life of the centers of
capitalistic enterprise during the sixteenth century. In this connection it is noteworthy that towns like Lyons and Antwerp
should have gone over so strongly to the new religious ideas.
In a word, Max Weber's theory is partly true; but it takes
into account only one aspect of the situation.[10]

On the other hand, it is certain that the expansion of capitalism contributed to the flowering of the Renaissance. It was
not the wealth and luxury alone which permitted the Mæ-
cenases of that day to encourage the arts; the independence of
spirit which the new economic organization favored should
also be taken into account. The artist, unrestrained by guild
regulations, was left remarkably free to pursue his work. The
more active trade relations between the different countries
imparted a greater freedom to the spirit. Thus, individualism
came into play at every point, whether we consider the progress of capitalism or the development of the Renaissance and
the Reformation. And, indeed, certain strong figures stood
out in sharp relief even in those days—striking personalities
like Jacob Fugger the Rich who freely imposed his terms upon
the proudest sovereigns of his age.

CHAPTER IV

CAPITALISM IN THE SIXTEENTH CENTURY: MARITIME COMMERCE AND COLONIAL EXPANSION

I. ECONOMIC CONSEQUENCES OF THE GREAT DISCOVERIES

THE most fruitful sources of modern capitalism, without doubt, have been the great maritime discoveries which began with the expeditions of the Portuguese into the Indian Ocean. Portugal was the first to establish flourishing settlements in India and to obtain a footing in Java, Sumatra, and the Moluccas. Then came the discovery of America, and its subsequent conquest, notably by Spain, which, together with Portugal was the principal maritime power of the Atlantic peoples during the sixteenth century. The opening up of the New World made further contribution to the growth of capitalism, for the early explorers and navigators were seeking direct contact with the countries producing cotton, silk, spices, and sugar, commodities already entering into current consumption, as well as with the sources of products previously unknown, such as dyewoods and cabinet woods, indigo, coffee, and tobacco.

In the main, however, the early colonial commercial operations meant the exploitation of primitive peoples who were incapable of defending themselves against the armaments of the invaders, as Werner Sombart well says. The first European traders realized enormous profits, sometimes in excess of 200 or 300 per cent, from dealings that were little less than piracy. Another source of profit, not less lucrative, was the forced

labor which the European peoples exacted of the natives in
their colonies. Spaniards, Portuguese, and Dutch alike showed
themselves pitiless toward their red or yellow subjects. Then,
as the native populations of America died off, it became necessary to import negroes from Africa, especially into the Antilles. The slave trade, despicable though it was, must be recognized as bringing in enormous profits. Therefore it was one
of the important sources of capitalism, however tainted.[1] Very
justly does Sombart say: "We have become rich because whole
races, whole peoples have died for us; for us continents have
been depopulated." Innumerable bits of evidence show that
the colonial commerce and the exploitation of the native
populations added enormously to the flood of wealth which
poured into Europe.

The existence of this lucrative commerce led to the perfect-
ing of established commercial practices, to the development
of new trade methods, and to the creation of an elaborate
maritime code. In good part, this was the work of Portuguese men of business, though the Spaniards imitated their
immediate predecessors. But the Portuguese (a great number
of whom—the so-called *marans*—were of Jewish origin, more
or less well converted to Catholicism) were the first to exploit
the new sources of wealth.[2]

II. THE PORTUGUESE AND SPANIARDS AT ANTWERP

Such an explanation would account for the great importance
of the Antwerp establishments of the Portuguese and Spaniards, at least until around 1560. Vessels of those nations entered the port of the Scheldt in great numbers. Antwerp became the great meeting place—especially the meeting place
of the nationals of the maritime powers, which were then
engaged in transporting both the products of Asia and the
New World, and those of the Northwest and North of Eu-

rope. Goods destined for the Spanish peninsula and the New World passed by way of Antwerp; and, of course, the trade in the products of the Low Countries—woolen cloth, linen, tapestries, religious objects, and works of art—centered here.

Important as Antwerp became, however—and no city had yet held so prominent a place—her economic activity would appear quite insignificant if compared with the commercial life of the present day. The ships of the day were small, their tonnage rarely exceeded 200 tons; and, though there were *caravels* of 300 to 500 tons, the light and sturdy *hulques* of not over 110 tons were preferred for the southern commerce. The number of sailings, while seeming enormous in those times, would also seem very small today: in the year 1542, there were only 36 sailings from Antwerp, destined for Spain. Yet in 1545, the merchandise exported through the port of Antwerp had a value of nearly 6 million *livres*—a very considerable figure for those times—whereas exports from the rest of the Low Countries were valued at only 2 million *livres*. It has been well remarked by Henri Pirenne that the Low Countries had become the suburbs of Antwerp. The merchandise imports, on the other hand, were largely colonial products.

The Portuguese colony (*nation*) at Antwerp occupied a particularly important place, although it numbered only about 70 families in 1570. This colony included two consuls who possessed authority to exercise consular jurisdiction over certain classes of disputes, under a scheme of procedure which was both expeditious and inexpensive. Obviously, this created a condition especially favorable to the business interests of the colony. Moreover, there was a representative of the King of Portugal at Antwerp, a factor who administered the commercial affairs of his sovereign. The Spanish colony at Antwerp was not a legally constituted *nation;* but, though the Spaniards had no officials with special powers of jurisdiction as had the Portuguese, they did in fact enjoy

certain other important privileges. Usually the Portuguese
and Spanish men of business were only commercial agents,
representing important firms of the countries of the South.
Apparently these agents acted both as brokers and financial
agents, at least until around 1550; but in the second half of
the century, there developed a differentiation of function.

III. THE GOLD AND SILVER OF THE NEW WORLD

The progress of commercial activity was not the only influence bringing about the expansion of capitalism during
the sixteenth century. Still another phenomenon played a
rôle of the first order, especially in the latter half of the
century. This was the enormous influx of the precious metals,
gold and silver, which had become very rare at the end of
the fifteenth and the beginning of the sixteenth century. Did
not Louis XII, in his decree of September 22, 1506, com-
plain that the exportation of gold and silver was raising the
price of these metals "to the very great prejudice and dam-
age" of his kingdom?

The West Coast of Africa first yielded a large quantity
of gold to the Portuguese; but the decisive factors, in this
particular, were the conquests of Mexico (1519–1527) and
Peru (1532–1541). The *conquistadores* shamelessly pillaged
the treasure stores which they found there; the treasure of
the Incas alone brought millions to Pizarro and his companions. In addition, tribute was exacted from the natives by
the Spaniards, who took possession of the country; and,
finally, regular revenues accrued from the mines. In 1545
came the discovery of Potosi—a rich silver mine with an
annual yield of 300,000 kilograms, some 10,000,000 troy
ounces. Mexico, New Granada, Peru, and (in lesser degree)
Chile poured forth quantities of gold and silver, to increase

the stock of the precious metals. In a single century, the output of these metals multiplied enormously; that of silver
nearly quintupled in the hundred years from 1520 to 1620.
Four-fifths of the new gold and silver came from Spanish
America.[3]

When Spain sought to maintain a monopoly control over
all this wealth, the effort failed, for the economic forces were
stronger than all her laws and institutions. In reality the
new treasure brought more profit to the other maritime powers
than to Spain; and the Spanish colonial system contributed to
her ruin.

IV. THE COLONIAL SYSTEM OF SPAIN

First of all, how did the Spanish monarchy propose to regulate the commerce of America? Not only did Spain seek to
reserve all this commerce to herself; but also, in order to make
control easier, she sought to concentrate it in a single port:
first, at Seville, and then, as the necessities of navigation required, at Cadiz, which is better situated than the capital of
Andalusia. The other Spanish ports naturally protested
against this exclusive monopoly and Charles V showed himself sympathetic with their claims; but, beginning with 1574,
under Philip II, the cause of Seville triumphed. Then Cadiz
competed with her and carried the day.

The organization which regulated all the trade with Spain
was the *Casa de contratación*. Created in 1502, it was located
first at Seville and then Cadiz, where it was established per-
manently. It was mainly a commercial institution, but it also
possessed jurisdiction over both criminal and civil actions
arising out of the trade with America. At the head were three
officials, who possessed great authority: the treasurer, the
factor or business manager, and the comptroller and secre-

tary (*contador*). But the operation of the *Casa*, like that of the whole Spanish administration, was hindered by "red tape."

Merchandise transported from Cadiz to Spanish America or from America to Spain was subjected to heavy duties (the *avería* of 2.5 per cent and the *almojarifazgo*). In the administration of the tax regulations the cargoes were registered, and the necessary entries made on the books of the comptroller. But the contraband trade grew to great proportions and these measures proved to be partly in vain. In 1660, therefore, the duties were replaced by a fixed sum of 790,000 ducats, paid by the merchants.

The Spanish king aimed to reserve for himself the greater part, if not the whole, of the precious metals from America; in reality, however, only a small part of this wealth entered the royal treasury. The Spanish government also fixed extremely heavy taxes on commercial transactions in the Indies and on the imports of goods and precious metals (*retours*) from America; but again only a small part of the sums due was received, for here again fraud and corruption played their part. In principle, also, only Spaniards had the right to settle in America. But, in this respect, too, many frauds were committed; and, furthermore, the number of Spaniards who established themselves in the Indies was relatively small, in view of the expanse of the regions under Spanish control.

Spain occupied a peculiar situation among the maritime powers. During the sixteenth century, she alone, with Portugal, possessed vast colonial territories; she had taken possession of a whole vast continent. Accordingly she could not enforce strictly what has been called the *colonial* system. Intercolonial trade, for example, while forbidden in principle, was in fact suffered to continue, since it could not be prevented.

On the other hand, Spain did struggle to retain the monopoly of trade with her colonies, much as did all the other colonial powers. But it is hard to imagine more absurd commercial practices than those which it was sought to enforce. Thus, the whole colonial commerce was to be concentrated in a single Spanish port, Cadiz, which was to have the monopoly of that commerce; and, in the New World, goods were to be landed at Vera Cruz, when destined for Mexico, and at Carthagena and Porto Bello when destined for much of South America. A French Memoir of 1691 on the commerce of Cadiz clearly describes the character of this trade and the machinery whereby it was carried on:

The galleons, in the first place, land at Carthagena. As soon as they arrive, the general of the galleons sends notice to the viceroy of Peru, who has his residence at Lima. . . . The viceroy immediately makes the news known to all the merchants, and gives the necessary orders for the transportation of the gold and silver to be sent to Panama by sea and from there to Porto Bello on mules.

The galleons usually remain four months at Carthagena, to trade there and exchange part of their merchandise. The trade done there amounts to about 4 million crowns. From Carthagena, the galleons go to Porto Bello, where a fair which lasts fifty or sixty days is then held; they leave European merchandise amounting to 18 or 20 million crowns there and bring back about 25 millions of crowns in gold, silver, and other merchandise of the country. From Porto Bello they return to Carthagena, where they stay fifteen days more, and from there they go to Havana, where they stay about the same time . . .

The fleets go to Vera Cruz, city of the kingdom of Mexico, where they usually unload all their cargo; and the merchants sell the goods there or transport them elsewhere if they wish. They remain in this port from the month of September until the month of June, when they leave again for Cadiz. . . .

The Spaniards also did business in the region of the Pampas, using the port of Buenos Aires; and, finally, they began to use the route to the Pacific via Cape Horn, though this route was used mainly in an illicit trade with the West Coast.

V. THE COMMERCE OF FOREIGNERS IN SPANISH AMERICA

The commerce with Spanish America was, in fact, mainly carried on by foreigners—at least indirectly, and principally by traders from the maritime nations of Northwest Europe. These powers had pushed ahead wonderfully toward the end of the sixteenth century and in the first half of the seventeenth, at the expense of Spain. Thus, England came to occupy an important place in the colonial trade and Holland proved even more important; for, as an outcome of the successful revolt against the Spanish monarchy, Holland had seized the fine colonial empire formerly controlled by Portugal. France held only third place, but the enterprising spirit of her Atlantic shipowners and sailors already promised to make her a formidable rival of Spain. Such, therefore, were the new economic and political forces which came into play in the sixteenth century, and which contributed in important degree to the extension of maritime commerce and commercial capitalism.

To be sure, the Dutch, English, and French could not engage openly in a direct trade with Spanish America; they must still use the port of Cadiz for a good part of their business. Accordingly, they sent their merchandise by sea to this port; but, in order to avoid the customs duties (sometimes as much as 23 per cent) fraudulent shipments were usually made. The Memoir of 1691, already cited, states that, out of 51 or 53 million *livres* of merchandise leaving Cadiz, 50 millions belonged to French, English, Dutch, Genoese, and Flemish traders. These either traded in the name of someone else (who lent his name for that purpose) or in the names of Spanish commission agents.

Under this guise, the French sent textiles, laces, silks, and especially linens, which constituted the principal article of the St.-Malo trade. This same Memoir of 1691 estimates that the following amounts were received by foreigners for goods shipped to America: the French, 13 or 14 million *livres;* the English, 6 or 7 millions; the Dutch, some 10 millions; citizens of Hamburg, some 4 millions; Genoese, 11 or 12 millions; and the Flemish, some 6 millions. Thus the Spaniards served mainly as carriers, while the other countries of Europe furnished the manufactured objects needed by the Spanish colonies. France was also sending great quantities of merchandise to Spain, and a considerable number of French artisans of various crafts settled in that country.[4]

VI. THE INFLUX OF THE PRECIOUS METALS AND THE MONETARY CRISIS

The precious metals began to flow steadily over Europe as early as the sixteenth century; and France was so overrun by the Spanish silver and gold that she suffered a monetary revolution, the consequences of which were extremely grave. First of all, the cutting down of the weight of the *livre tournois*, a unit of account, is to be noted. This action aggravated the depreciation in the purchasing power of money. Also, an attempt was made, by the Edict of September 1577, to prevent the circulation of coins of other countries; but this effort proved vain. Foreign coins, especially Spanish coins—worth less than similar French coins—invaded France, while the French money flowed out of the country. A result of this condition was an unbridled speculation in exchange, which enriched the financiers and the bankers, and led numerous merchants to abandon their commercial pursuits to undertake banking and exchange operations.

This influx of the precious metals and the speculation in

foreign exchange set into operation the rise of prices which marks the sixteenth century, and especially the second half of that century. The rise in grain prices was most noticeable, but it was appreciable also for many valuable materials and manufactured products. Land rents and the price of land also rose. Even in the French countryside, there was an active speculation in land and in the products of agriculture. A class of laborer-merchants grew up, who sometimes became wealthy enough to buy numbers of farms and even noble fiefs, in imitation of the merchants of the towns. This occurred at the very time when members of the old nobility, ruined by the rise of prices, were selling lands, and thus finding themselves precipitated into an inferior position, if the favor of the Court failed to "regild" their coats-of-arms.[5]

It is difficult to determine the extent of the price advance in France. It seems to have been not less than 100 per cent, and may have been 200 per cent. The royal administration tried to remedy the rise by fixing *maxima* for prices and wages, notably by Edicts published in 1554, 1567, and 1577; but such efforts proved vain. Only a few contemporaries understood the true causes of the phenomenon, notably Jean Bodin, who published his *Discours sur le rehaussement et la diminution des monnaies* at Paris in 1578.[6]

Moreover, these phenomena were not peculiar to France. The rise of prices occurred everywhere in Europe, during the sixteenth century, and especially in the second half of the century. It was felt in England, where it contributed to the increase of the manorial rents. Another consequence of the inflow of the precious metals was the accumulation of wealth in other forms than landed property, such forms, for example, as merchandise and money. This stimulated a great outburst of economic activity, which was first reflected in the expansion of commerce, and then in the development of new industries.

This greater accumulation of wealth in the hands of individuals also gave rise to new economic ideas, as developed in the mercantilist and protective system. This fact explains the efforts to establish colonies which should be at once the outlet for the products of the mother country and the source of metals and precious commodities. It also explains the colonial system, the aim of which was to assure a monopoly of trade to the mother country.

VII. THE ECONOMIC PROGRESS OF THE MARITIME
POWERS

A. FRANCE—The outstanding development of the latter half of the sixteenth century is the progress of the maritime powers of the West and Northwest of Europe. These were destined to succeed to the position earlier held by Portugal and Spain.

Here the rôle of France is destined to be one of secondary importance, albeit a very honorable rôle. There was a considerable expansion of the French foreign commerce—principally the trade with Spain (a country which had need of the products of France and which could pay only in specie) and also that with England, which eagerly sought the agricultural produce of France.

To be sure, France still looked toward the East: she concluded an understanding with the Mamelukes of Egypt, and then in 1536 she signed *capitulations* with the Sultan. These recognized her protectorate over all the Catholics in the Ottoman Empire. No longer having the competition of Venice to fear, France became the foremost maritime power in the Mediterranean.

Still, the French did not neglect the New World. They took part in numerous expeditions to Newfoundland, to Brazil, to Guiana, and to the coast of North America. Jacques Cartier explored Canada between 1534 and 1541. The French were not successful in establishing themselves in Brazil and Florida, but they did participate in the illicit commerce with South America. Le Havre was created under Francis I and the prosperity of ports like Nantes and Bordeaux dates from the sixteenth century.

B. HOLLAND—As early as the sixteenth century, Holland showed signs, even more clearly than did France, that she was destined to be a great maritime power. Dutch shipyards were already famous, and well before their revolt against the Spanish monarchy, the Low Countries of the North had possessed a merchant marine of the first order, which came to play a more and more important rôle at Antwerp. Indeed, their merchants had displaced those of the Hanseatic towns in the Baltic and had obtained a great part of that trade.

Even during the war against Spain, the trade of the Dutch with that country was never completely interrupted. Nor was it less lucrative because carried on illegally and in secret; indeed, at this very time Holland turned to trading with Cadiz, and thus opened up the flow of precious metals which were to build up her own enormous monetary stock. This is shown by an interesting memoir dated 1607:

> The traffic and navigation carried on in Spain by the said rebels in the past were under the cover of France, England, and Germany; and by this Spanish trade during the past 22 years, the rebels have brought back much silver and gold to their towns and provinces in exchange for cheeses, wheat, butter, herrings, various kinds of manufactured goods, meat, beer, tar, wax, and other merchandise from Oostlande (from the Baltic). By this means, they have acquired still greater treasures than they could by their fishing and the Oostlande navigation; and with great dissimulation and deceit they have made it appear (by means of false certifications and passports, counterfeited by deputies whom they have for this purpose) that they were from Denmark, Oostlande, and Norway, and subjects of the Germanic Empire.[7]

The revolt against Spain had another fortunate consequence for the maritime and colonial commerce of Holland.
The annexation of Portugal by Philip II in 1580 meant that
the Dutch could no longer turn to Lisbon for supplies of the
spices and precious commodities of the Far East. Therefore
they undertook to seek out a way to India and the islands of
the Indian Ocean in order to obtain such supplies. Gradually,
indeed, they acquired the settlements and colonies of the
Portuguese and took over this very lucrative trade. The
growth of the commerce with the East explains the creation
of the Dutch East India Company at the beginning of the
seventeenth century.

C. ENGLAND—Not until the second half of the sixteenth century did the English really begin to participate in
the great overseas trade. This development was greatly encouraged by the nationalistic policy of the Tudor government,
which, finding itself in great need for money, sought means
for increasing the economic resources of the nation. Under
Elizabeth, therefore, a strongly nationalistic policy was inaugurated.

At this point, the efforts of Burleigh to develop the maritime power of England are most significant. In order to develop a body of good sailors, he encouraged fishing, applauded
the exploits of the privateers, and even authorized the contraband slave trade.[8] He also encouraged the cultivation of
hemp and flax, the manufacture of sail cloths, and the production of ship timbers. He ordered a thorough survey of the
ports and had important works undertaken for their repair
—all steps designed to encourage the development of shipping.

In the effort to expand their maritime commerce, the English also worked to open new markets. Here a characteristic
development was the progress achieved by the Company of
Merchant Adventurers.[9] The Teutonic Hanse had been ex-

pelled from London in 1597, once for all; but, despite this action, the English Company was able to establish itself at Hamburg in 1611. Once established in Hamburg, it was able to attract a noteworthy part of the trade of Germany.

Not less characteristic of the nationalistic policy was the creation of new privileged companies. In 1554, the Muscovy Company, which may be considered as the first great stock company, was chartered and presently controlled an important part of the commerce of Russia. In 1579 came the Eastland Company, formed to undertake trade in the Baltic, which was soon to feel the victorious competition of the Dutch. The Levant Company was formed in 1581. This did not confine its operations to the Mediterranean; but by 1584 had pushed East as far as Goa in India. Lastly, there was the Hudson's Bay Company—an enterprise destined to maintain itself to the present day. The fur trade brought in fine profits to this company.

The English also tried to find a northeast passage and to reach the Far East. The expeditions of Willoughby and Chancellor resulted in the discovery of the White Sea and the establishment of Archangel. In the main, however, it was the struggle against the Spaniards which proved most fruitful. In this respect, there is nothing so important as the expeditions to America undertaken by Drake, from 1577 to 1580. Drake rounded Cape Horn, pillaged the Pacific Coast, and then sailed westward to escape from the enemy fleets. He brought home a treasure worth at least a million and a half pounds sterling—a treasure consisting of gold, silver, and pearls. This was an enormous sum when we consider that the expedition cost only £5000, and that it comprised only four small boats, with a total tonnage of 375 tons, manned by 160 men.[10] Up to the end of the sixteenth century, the English privateers continued their attacks on Spanish vessels and on the ports and colonies of their enemies. The destruction of the Invincible Armada, in 1588, still further increased their daring; and, by the year 1600, the maritime destiny of England was very clearly foreshadowed.

All these overseas expeditions appear to have contributed powerfully to the accumulation of capital by the nations of Western Europe. The consequence was an increase of their political power; and it is easy to understand why France, England, and Holland held first place in the Europe of the seventeenth century. Unfortunately, the amount of the capital accumulations cannot be determined with anything like numerical accuracy. Therefore we are forced to fall back on the rise of prices—which manifested itself in all these countries—as the best index of the change.

VIII. THE ORIGIN OF JOINT STOCK COMPANIES

In the second half of the sixteenth century, and at the beginning of the seventeenth, there developed a new economic institution of great importance—the joint stock company.[11] England here led the way. A beginning was made when the Merchant Adventurers, who had first begun operations at the opening of the fifteenth century, formed a commercial company. But this was a sort of guild, such as had existed formerly in England, and the company did not trade with a collective capital: each of the merchants who composed its membership traded with his own individual capital and for his own account.

Not until 1553 did a number of these *adventurers* form the "mysterie and Companie of the Marchants Adventurers for the discovery of regions, dominions, islands and places unknown." Actually, trade with Muscovy was intended. Since considerable expeditions—which would prove both costly and difficult—were to be fitted out, something more than the enterprise of individuals was needed. The traders were to penetrate the White Sea; and, after they had landed at their warehouse at Archangel, they must still traverse hundreds of miles into the heart of Russia. Therefore they created a real stock company, with a capital of 240 shares of 25 pounds sterling each. However, the joint effort was limited to a single voyage; and after each voyage the profits were shared in proportion to the capital which each of the associates had invested. It was not until later that the corporation assumed a permanent character. The English companies, formed at the end of the sixteenth century, continued to resemble the Muscovy Company. Moreover, development of this new business institution to its highest degree of perfection was to be the contribution of Holland.

CHAPTER V

COMMERCIAL AND FINANCIAL CAPITALISM IN THE SEVENTEENTH CENTURY

I. THE DESTRUCTION OF THE SPANISH COMMERCIAL MONOPOLY IN AMERICA

D URING the seventeenth century, the Spanish monopoly of commerce with the colonies in America steadily grew weaker. More and more, the profits of trade with the New World escaped from Spain and fell into the hands of more energetic powers—Holland, England, and France. This is one of the most significant changes marking the evolution of capitalism during the seventeenth century.

In the course of this shift of financial and commercial power, Amsterdam became the great money market of Europe. This result was due mainly to the extensive Dutch commerce with Spain, and especially the trade with Cadiz. This trade, which had been maintained during the war, became much more active after 1648, when it became more important than the Spanish trade of France and England. By the end of the century, thirty to fifty Dutch ships were engaged in transporting precious metals and specie; and these carried away more than half of the treasure arriving at Cadiz. The success of the Dutch in supplanting the French in this trade after the close of the Dutch war (1672–1678) is evidenced in the following statement written by Huet, Bishop of Avranches, in his contemporary memorandum on the trade of Holland:

The Spaniards have favored the commerce of the Dutch as much as possible, particularly since the year 1667, with a view to diminishing ours. In this effort they have not been unsuccessful. The trade of the Dutch has never been so flourishing as since the Dutch war of 1672 up to the beginning of that now being waged (the War of the Spanish Succession), for the Dutch then furnished a good part of the merchandise which we had been accustomed to carry to Spain and took in exchange quantities of the merchandise which they had been accustomed to obtain in France before this war of 1672 and that of 1690.

As a result of this trade, the monetary stock of Holland became so considerable that she was able to export both metals and specie, not only to India, in the course of trade with that country, but to several countries of Europe, quite contrary to the regulations of the mercantile system.

Furthermore, the Dutch, English, and French had carried on an illicit trade in Spanish America, as early as the sixteenth century, in addition to the trade by way of Cadiz. This illegal traffic developed still further in the next century, and especially in the latter half of that century. How this could develop, contrary to law, is readily understood when the extent of the coast line, and especially the avarice of the Spanish governors, are taken into account. In the latter half of the century the French, English, and Dutch established themselves firmly in the Antilles, close to America, at Martinique, at Guadeloupe, at Jamaica, and at Curaçao. Thereafter, the illicit trade became still more active, though the English and Dutch had the start of the French in this business. In 1662, when the Spanish galleons reached American mainland, they found the markets so well supplied that they had to carry back the greatest part of their cargoes.[1]

The "foreigners" approached a colonial port and then asked to have their vessels repaired there, winning over the governor by making presents to him. That the trick was turned in this fashion is shown by Huet in the work cited above:

> The Dutch have even found a way to trade secretly there (in America), or, to state it better, directly by means of the island of Curaçao, which is not far from the city of Carthagena. The merchants of this famous city and of some others on the seacoast have an understanding with the Dutch, by which they carry their merchandise to the ships while the latter are at anchor at some convenient place on the coast. This merchandise they exchange for European goods.

Then, toward the end of the seventeenth century, the South Seas (the coasts of the Pacific) attracted the cupidity of the foreigners, notably the French, and above all those from St.-Malo, who made superb profits there. In some years this trade brought in more than 200 million *livres*.[2] Finally, there was the Philippine commerce which was enormously profitable, sometimes netting as much as 600 per cent. In part, this trade also escaped from the hands of the mother country.

Thus, the commercial monopoly in her colonies, which Spain sought to hold for herself, was practically broken down, especially in the eighteenth century. By the Treaty of Utrecht, England obtained the *asiento*, opening the slave trade to the English and also giving the right to maintain a *vaisseau de permission*.[3]

Thus, the Spaniards allowed this rich source of wealth to slip through their fingers. Yet though they did not know how to profit for themselves—or, at least, though they profited only in a very slight measure from the immense resources of their magnificent colonial empire—the failure was not due solely to lack of effort. Nor was it due to economic incapacity, nor to corrupt administrators, whether in high or low position. Other factors are to be taken into account: notably the very nature of the Spanish peninsula, more African than Euro-

pean, partly barren, divided into natural compartments between which it is very difficult to maintain communication.
Do not "geographic conditions condemn a part of the surface
of Spain to an almost irremediable agricultural poverty"?
Therefore, is it quite just to speak of the economic decadence
of Spain? Has not her economic strength always been small?
The products of her agriculture were, taken together, scanty;
and her industrial life had developed only slightly.

Spain, even though better governed, would not have been
able to hold mastery of the commerce with her overseas
colonies. Since she had not the goods needed by her colonies,
the possibilities of exchange with them were limited. Thus,
the failure of Spain was due not alone to the easy-going dis-
position of the Spanish people, nor to their absorption in the
business of fighting, after the long crusade against the Turks.
Clearly, also, the expulsion of the Moors and Jews does not
explain the incapacity of Spain to improve the immense
colonies which she had conquered. And finally, one fact stands
out clearly: the inflow of the precious metals, which Spain
could not keep and use for economic ends, was fatally detri-
mental to her welfare.

II. THE MERCANTILIST POLICY

The inflow of the precious metals into Europe led to the
development of the mercantilist policy, or at least contributed
in considerable measure to that development. The mercantilist
theory triumphed everywhere in the seventeenth century.
Even Colbert instituted his strongly protective system in order to attract as much money as possible to France and to
prevent specie from going outside the Kingdom. On the same
grounds, he struggled bitterly against the commercial supremacy of Holland; and he applied himself energetically and
perseveringly to the creation of a manufacturing industry in

Jean Baptiste Colbert
Secretaire et Ministre d'Estat

France: "The manufactures are producing returns in money which is the sole end of trade and the sole means of increasing the grandeur and power of the state." Nor was Colbert the only one to wish to decrease the wages of labor; and in England, as in France, attempts were made to lower interest rates. Moreover, the English Navigation Acts of 1651 and 1660 had preceded the famous French protective tariffs of 1664 and 1667, and thus had contributed to England's ability to outdistance France.

The inflow of specie was everywhere looked upon, not only as a source of prosperity for individuals, but also as an essential condition for increasing the power of the state. Did not that loyal Englishman, Thomas Mun, in his *England's Treasure by Foreign Trade*,[4] attribute the enormous powers of the kings of Spain and the House of Austria to the treasures of the Indies? Colbert's views were much the same.

This mercantilist conception (which is destined to be fought so vigorously by the liberal school during the eighteenth century) had, it must be granted, a real reason for existence, at a time when commercial and financial capitalism was still in its adolescence. Commercial relations between European powers were still but little developed, and each country was, as one might say, sufficient unto itself. The progress of commerce and capitalism brings about a change of this condition, and with it the destruction of the mercantilist system.

III. THE COMMERCIAL AND FINANCIAL SUPREMACY OF HOLLAND

Another characteristic of the seventeenth century is the steady shift of economic activity toward the Northwest.

Holland was the first country to usurp the place of Spain and Portugal, the original great maritime powers. The su-

premacy of Holland was ensured by the outcome of the struggle against the Spanish monarchy, which was then in control
of Portugal; for the Dutch acquired the important Portuguese settlements in India, and the rich islands of the East
Indies, notably Java and Sumatra, and the Moluccas, or Spice
Islands. During the whole of the seventeenth century, therefore, Holland held a position of recognized commercial supremacy; and, because agriculture and even industry played
only a secondary rôle in the economic activity of the Dutch,
Holland stood out as a sort of symbol of commercial and
financial capitalism.

Her dominant position in the East meant that Holland
was able to obtain the spices so much sought after in that
day (notably pepper, of which she had the monopoly) direct
from the islands of the Indian Ocean. Holland alone was able
to obtain the right to maintain a trading post in Japan; and
she also succeeded in capturing part of the China trade, although the ports of the Celestial Empire had not yet been
opened for direct trade with Europeans. As a result of these
achievements, the Dutch ports, notably Amsterdam, became
the marts to which the world turned for supplies of the products from the Far East.

Furthermore,—and in spite of the efforts of England,—
Holland possessed almost a monopoly of the Baltic commerce; she also controlled a very important trade in wheat.
The greater part of this grain she transported to the countries
of the south of Europe and, in times of high prices, even to
France. Her business with France, Spain, and the Levant was
also very considerable, and her business men regularly carried on the French trade with the countries of the North. She
failed to conquer Brazil, which continued in the hands of the
Portuguese, but she did acquire the colony of Surinam in
Guiana; and possession of the island of Curaçao gave her

the necessary base for carrying on the illicit trade with America.

The superiority of the Dutch fleet and the scale of her shipping operations gave Holland the lowest freight rates of those times. Thus, with her own resources, she was in a position to maintain a very active exchange of goods between the Far East and all the Western world. Indeed, she had only to establish herself strongly in America in order to defy all competition for a long time to come. Her strength in these particulars explains the astonishing success of the Dutch in the commission trade, against which Colbert tried to struggle, though without much result; not until the wars at the end of the reign of Louis XIV was the Dutch position impaired.

IV. THE DUTCH EAST INDIA COMPANY AND THE BANK OF AMSTERDAM

Her strong position in the world of trade, together with the considerable monetary stock which she had accumulated, made Holland the greatest financial power in Europe. Two institutions of fundamental importance, the Dutch East India Company and the Bank of Amsterdam, contributed greatly to this position. The East India Company, founded in 1602, received the monopoly of the trade in the East Indies for 19 years; and this monopoly power was regularly renewed thereafter.

This company was a real corporation of the modern type. Its original capital of 600,000 florins was increased gradually to 6,300,000 florins. The value of each of the 2,100 shares (3,000 florins par value) had grown to 16,950 florins in 1699; and the dividends often amounted to 15 and even 25 per cent. The company also issued bonds for the sum of 12,600,000 florins, bearing interest at 3½ per cent.

Necessarily, the value of the shares in the company fluctuated with changes in trade conditions and the political outlook; and they became the medium of a continuous speculation. Outright purchases for cash occurred and there was also a considerable credit or "future" business in the shares. Thus a contemporary Memoir says, "It is possible to do a big business without having shares or even the desire to acquire any; and indeed there has never been any greater business." Speculative trading of this kind could be undertaken the more safely, because, by payment of premiums, the risks could be made almost insignificant, sometimes as little as two per cent. In addition, as the Memoir adds, there was a variety of other devices; and those who engaged in the traffic were necessarily quick and clever people, "whose first interests were to color the news and to invent a thousand devices for gaining their desired end." Spreading false news was a game much played on the *bourse*.[5]

The administration of the East India Company resembled that of a state. There were the Directors, an Assembly of Seventeen, and the General of the Indies, who administered the affairs of the company in the East. There was also a corps of well paid functionaries—though the mere fact that these subordinates were well paid did not keep them from violating their trust occasionally and looking out for their own interests, to the detriment of those of the Company. Nevertheless, it must be recognized that the organization of the East India Company served as a model for most of the privileged trading companies formed in other countries during the seventeenth and eighteenth centuries.

No less remarkable was the organization of the Bank of Amsterdam,[6] which was founded in 1608 by the City Council. Its place of business was the city hall. Thus the Bank of Amsterdam had the character of a true government institution, since it operated under the authority of the city magistrates. Its routine operations were carried on by subordinate officers (guards, bookkeepers, cashiers, and the like) who were sworn to obey the city authorities, and pledged to keep secret everything relative to the condition of the bank.

The original funds of the Bank consisted of *bank money* (*argent de banque*). The Bank did not issue bank notes, however; nor was it, properly speaking, a credit institution. It received specie on deposit, but the total amount of such deposits was not retained in its vaults, but instead a part was devoted to uses which would bring in an income. Almost from the first, substantial advances were made to the East India Company and even to the City of Amsterdam. The Bank also profited from the pawnbroking operations of its *lombard*, a sort of pawnshop where the borrowers paid from 6 to 20 per cent of the value of the objects pledged. But the Bank was intended to operate mainly in the exchange market; and it was established with the aim of displacing the private money changers whose operations were considered harmful. It was essentially a *giro* or exchange bank. Drafts from foreign countries on Amsterdam and Amsterdam drafts on foreign countries were settled at the bank, as also were the transactions of the East India Company. It is noteworthy that merchandise was sold at lower prices when payment was to be made at the bank. Bank money came to be worth five per cent more than the specie generally current (variations in the value of which fixed what was called the *agio*).

There were almost always over 2,000 depositors of the Bank, and business men generally had funds on deposit with the Bank, a "bank account." The method of using these deposits is described in the Memoir previously quoted. "When a private individual wishes to pay over some part of his account to anyone," says this contemporary account, "he must carry the check himself or give power of attorney before the bookkeepers to the person whom he wishes to authorize to carry his check." Moreover, the Bank came to play an outstanding rôle in the commercial life of the time. "To have credit," states the Memoir, "you must have an account at the bank, and you must pay or receive in this way if you wish to keep your credit." In a word, "this bank is without contradiction the most considerable which has ever existed, and there are no private individuals in Europe, if their trade extends to these provinces at all, who are not interested directly or indirectly in it, often without knowing it." The extent of the financial power of the Bank is indicated by the fact that after the end of the seventeenth century, and during almost the whole of the eighteenth century, its cash on hand exceeded 20,000,000 florins. Several times it held a great part of the French currency, notably at the time of the inflation of 1720 and again during the commercial crisis of 1763.

We readily understand, therefore, how Amsterdam became the great financial market of the world in the seventeenth century, and why it was destined to remain such during a good part of the eighteenth. There the great bulk of the bills were negotiated and exchange rates were established. All traders kept their eyes constantly fixed on Holland. As Werner Sombart well says, it was Holland which contributed most to the "commercializing" of economic life. Credit became "impersonal," an indispensable condition for the extension and triumph of capitalism, as well as for formation of a capitalistic attitude of mind.

Holland's example also shows the close relationship between the expansion of maritime commerce on a large scale and the appearance of the most characteristic institutions of capitalism, such as the business corporation and such operations as speculation in exchange and securities and dealing in futures.[7]

V. THE COMMERCIAL AND COLONIAL EXPANSION OF ENGLAND

Quite unlike Holland, seventeenth century England was far from being an exclusively commercial power. Manufacturing industry, notably the woolen industry, held an important place there, as we have already seen, though industry then contributed much less to the expansion of capitalism than did maritime and colonial commerce. None the less, toward the end of the seventeenth century, a great number of new companies were springing up in such diverse fields as the metallurgical industries, the textile industry, and the manufacture of paper.

By the beginning of the seventeenth century, moreover, England was attaining a position as a colonial power. Her first colonies in the Antilles were acquired at the expense of Spain: Barbados was occupied in 1605, the Bermudas in 1612, and Saint Christopher—possession of which completed the British holdings in the Caribbean—in 1622–24. Jamaica was added in 1655. The need for laborers in the sugar islands led naturally to establishment of slavery, and in 1618 the Guinea Company was organized to carry on the slave trade.

The English were not able to found colonies in South America; but in North America they planted a settlement in Virginia as early as the latter years of the sixteenth century. In 1606, King James I issued the patent under the great seal, generally called the first Virginia Charter, granting privileges to two groups, the London and Plymouth Companies.[8] Later came the New England settlements. The Pilgrims landed at Plymouth in 1620, and Boston was founded ten years later. Then, in 1667, Holland ceded New Amsterdam, which was renamed New York.

The English also made a vigorous drive toward the East Indies in the first half of the seventeenth century. In 1600 the first East India Company was founded; and in 1622 this was transformed into a corporation. Several settlements were established in India: Surate, in 1609; Madras, in 1639; Hougly, in 1650; and Bombay, in 1665. But the English were not able to dislodge the Dutch either from the islands of the Indian ocean or the Moluccas. Moreover, the political troubles which marked the reign of Charles I and the period of the Commonwealth, retarded the rate of England's maritime and colonial expansion. Holland profited by this unsettlement to impose her commercial supremacy on the world.

With the restoration of the Stuarts came the revival of England's commercial activity. While the Navigation Acts (the Act of 1660 more than that of 1651) perhaps reacted unfavorably on the English colonies in the East Indies, they did enable England to defend herself against the Dutch aggressions. In the interim, her great rival was being weakened to some extent by the wars of the time of Louis XIV, by the War of the League of Augsburg, and then, most of all, by the War of the Spanish Succession. The War of the League of Augsburg, to be sure, had caused great losses to British as well as Dutch commerce.

It is the Treaty of Utrecht, at the close of the War of the Spanish Succession (1713), which marks the beginning of the commercial and maritime prominence of England, however, or at least foreshadows it. At Utrecht, England obtained the privilege of the *asiento* and of the *vaisseau de permission*, which enabled her to capture a great part of the South American trade, at the very moment when France was obliged to give up the illicit trade on the Pacific Coast. Even earlier (1708), Chamberlayne—not without some exaggeration, to be sure—had said in his *Magnae Britanniae notitia:* "our commerce is the most considerable of the whole world."

The maritime expansion of England at the end of the six-teenth and in the seventeenth century gave another stimulus to financial capitalism. The privileged trading companies, dis-cussed above, all took on a capitalistic form and were or-ganized as stock companies. This was true, for example, of the Muscovy Company, of the Eastland Company, and of the African Company. The companies founded for the exploita-tion of the North American colonies were also great corpora-tions, the capital of which amounted to 300,000 pounds ster-ling in 1624, that of the Virginia Company alone representing 200,000 pounds. Altogether, there were some 140 stock com-panies—with an aggregate capital amounting to 4,250,000 pounds sterling—in England and Scotland at the end of the seventeenth century. Over three-fourths of this sum (3,232,-000 pounds) belonged to six enterprises: the East India Com-pany, the Guinea or African Company, the Hudson's Bay Company, the New River Company, the Bank of England, and the Million Bank.

The British East India Company, founded at the begin-ning of the seventeenth century, almost at the same mo-ment as the Dutch Company, was the greatest capitalistic or-ganization of them all. The shares of this great corporation were designated by the term *capital* and not by that of *stock*,[9] as had been the case with the Merchant Adventurers. Its divi-dends were very high from the beginning, exceeding 30 per cent; and an important speculation occurred in the shares of the East India Company in England, much as in Holland. There were, in fact, very severe fluctuations in the price of shares. Those of the East India Company fell from 200 pounds sterling, in 1692, to 37 in 1697; in the same interval, the shares of the Guinea Company fell from 52 to 13 pounds sterling, and those of the Hudson's Bay Company, from 260 to 80. Such fluctuations resulted from crises and above all from the reactions inevitably following a period of feverish speculation. It proved impossible to remedy this evil and even the conviction of a number of stock jobbers produced no effect.

Finally, the evolution of financial capitalism had been interrupted by a period of immobility caused by the civil war and the commercial depression, which followed in its train. With the Restoration there began a period of renaissance and expansion, both for commerce and for industry, which in turn reacted upon financial conditions. Around 1678–1680 supplies of credit developed to such a point that interest rates fell as low as 5 and even 4 per cent. The large commercial companies, notably the African and Hudson's Bay Companies, made considerable profits; and the East India Company made still higher profits, its dividends sometimes reaching 380 per cent.[10] In 1694 occurred a most significant event, the founding of a national bank, the Bank of England. This was an event of great importance in the evolution of English capitalism. Creation of the Bank brought into existence an institution which was to assure the credit standing of the new government which followed the Revolution of 1688.[11]

VII. THE SECONDARY RÔLE OF FRANCE

Developments in France were similar to those in contemporary England; but the growth of capitalism was much less vigorous there. Capitalism began to appear even in domestic commerce, however, though it is possible to appraise fairly only the progress accomplished in the wholesale trade. Such trade was undertaken by the wholesalers, the mercers and the drapers. This class furnished the theme for Jacques Savary's *Complete Man of Business* (*Le parfait négociant*) which

Paris Chez Claude Robustel rue St. Jacques a l'Image St. Jean.

treats mainly of the wholesale trade, showing its importance and drawing attention to the difficulties and risks involved. The men of business (*négociants*) came to form an entirely new class, the members of which might even enter the ranks of the nobility. They were freed from the heavy burdens imposed on the guilds, and became so important that they achieved places as judges in the tribunals of commerce (*tribunaux consulaires*). Jacques Savary testifies to all this.

Louis XIII, by his ordinance dated January 1627, permitted wholesale merchants to attain rank in the French nobility, and Louis XIV declared they need not abandon trade in order to be eligible for appointment as secretary to the King—a position conferring nobility on those who served in this office or who had so served for twenty years. It also brought a position in the nobility to all their direct descendants.[12]

It was the wholesale merchants, therefore, and particularly the mercers who, by acquiring considerable capital, tended to emerge from the rank and file of the guilds. The mercers sold all sorts of merchandise including linens, thread, ribbons, braids, belts and embroideries; and the variety of the goods they sold brought them into constant conflict with other trades. The drapers and booksellers, for example, disputed their right to sell alphabets and almanacs. Later on, the mercers were the first to establish novelty stores.

The mercers and drapers constituted the aristocracy of the merchant class. At Dijon, for example, because of their wealth, they constituted "even more than the members of the liberal professions, the intermediate class between the privileged group and the artisans." From this group of merchants, the personnel of the privileged trading companies was in part recruited; and from it, also, came the managers of the manufacturing industries. That they played a large part in the formation of the India Company is not surprising, therefore; nor is it astonishing that their subscriptions to the capital of that enterprise were very important.

The progress of French commerce was also marked by the development of a spirit of adventure and enterprise. Savary remarks that people were too hasty in their efforts to establish themselves on their own account and that they often acted imprudently: "In olden times, a man served twelve or fifteen or even twenty years before setting up in business on his own account. Therefore fewer bankruptcies and failures were witnessed in those times than now; and one can say, without fear of exaggeration, that more failures and bankruptcies have occurred in the last thirty or forty years than had taken place in a hundred years before." And Savary laid stress on the usefulness of a long period of apprenticeship.

Capitalism was destined to play only a secondary rôle in domestic trade, however; for the trade in farm products, and especially the grain trade, constituted the most important branches of commerce confined to the limits of the kingdom. Thus, in Languedoc—where the wine trade played a less considerable part than it does today, the only wines sold outside the province being brandies and wines of superior quality— the domestic trade had a value of about 1,200,000 *livres*. Moreover, it was not the custom to accumulate supplies of grain during the seventeenth century as later came to be the case; and finally, it is noteworthy that most of the towns, even the capitals of provinces, like Dijon and Rennes, remained purely local markets.

VIII. EXPANSION OF FRENCH COMMERCE OVERSEAS

In the field of foreign commerce, on the other hand, capitalism made real strides forward. Foreign commerce developed markedly during the seventeenth century, despite the handicaps imposed by the mercantilist system. This hindered its expansion in certain measure. Mercantilist regulations were in effect before the time of Colbert; but that great minister strengthened them greatly. The work of Colbert was not in vain, however, and trade with foreign countries made real progress during the reign of Louis XIV.[13]

A further fact, which at once reflects the growth of foreign trade, was the increasing importance of economic considerations in international affairs. After 1670, the great wars—not merely the Dutch war, but also the War of the League of Augsburg[14]—were in large part caused by economic rivalries; and commercial clauses therefore came to occupy a larger and larger place in the treaties of peace.

The advantages of foreign trade were by no means equally shared by the various countries,—and certainly French commerce worked out to the advantage of the foreign countries with which she traded more than to the advantage of France. In England, for example, French traders were subjected to annoyances which made dealings with that country very difficult. Here again we have the testimony of Savary: "There is no country in Europe where the French have more difficulty in carrying on their commerce and where they are more ill-treated than in England, yet there are none who receive and treat the English more generously than the French." To protect its manufacturers, the English government imposed prohibitive duties on the competitive French products. This meant that the French could export only their agricultural products to England; and even then the wheat, wine, and brandies of France could be shipped only in English boats through the ports of Bordeaux, La Rochelle, and Nantes.[15]

Similarly, the important trade with Holland was carried on almost entirely in Dutch ships; and the relatively prosperous trade with the Hanseatic towns and that with Muscovy were also in the hands of the Dutch. In 1669, Colbert created a *Compagnie du Nord* to engage in this trade; but, since the

French continued to turn their merchandise over to foreigners, France never succeeded in establishing direct trade relations even with Brandenburg. The trade with Spain (one of the best customers of France) was also largely in the hands of the Dutch. Nevertheless vessels from Nantes and St. Malo did go to Spain in fairly large numbers, especially to Bilbao and Cadiz.

The condition of the French trade with the Levant seems to have improved during the second half of the seventeenth century. Up to 1660, this trade had languished; but Colbert contributed to its restoration by establishing Marseilles as a free port. To be sure, the *Compagnie du Levant* failed to achieve the results which the minister had expected; but the general merchant trade with the East developed greatly toward the end of the century. The French surpassed the Dutch in this trade, though the English doubtless continued to hold first place. In 1713, merchandise from the Levant worth 11,-000,000 *livres* was unloaded at Marseilles; nearly 300 vessels were operated in this trade, and French merchants and consuls were to be found everywhere in the ports of the Ottoman Empire.

The colonial and maritime commerce proved very profitable; and the costly expeditions, with their attendant heavy risks, led those engaged in this trade to have recourse to formation of large corporations. It was recognized, moreover, that the capital at the command of an individual would be insufficient for a large scale enterprise necessarily attended by considerable risk. In fact, it was thought—and not without reason—that under the existing economic and political situation in Europe, only companies of this sort could undertake such a venture. Finally, the successes of the English East India Company and the Dutch Company (especially the dividends which they distributed) led the French to follow this example.

LE PARFAIT
NEGOCIANT

In 1664, Colbert endeavored to set up the *Compagnies des Indes Orientales* and *des Indes Occidentales*, though he experienced great difficulty in attracting the necessary capital. The East India Company (*Compagnie des Indes Orientales*) achieved a considerable measure of success, in spite of the great obstacles which it encountered; but the West India Company (*Compagnie des Indes Occidentales*) proved so unsuccessful that, in 1674, Colbert was forced to give up the attempt at monopoly and to allow others to participate in the trade of the Antilles, Canada and Acadia. The Senegal Company (*Compagnie du Sénégal*), created in 1673, achieved only an indifferent success, despite its participation in the slave trade. Establishment of large scale trading enterprises in France was attended with great difficulty, and Colbert's commercial policy in large part failed. The French were also unsuccessful in their efforts to supplant the Dutch, as is shown by his inability to dislodge the latter from their position of supremacy in the sugar trade. On the whole, the French men of business (*négociants*) seem to have preferred freedom for their trading operations, as is shown by the declarations of the deputies of commerce in 1701; and the colonists seem to have shared these sentiments.

Moreover, it holds true that the merchants preferred to venture the capital at their disposal in the colonial trade. This willingness is easily explained, for the colonial trade dealt in tropical commodities then so much sought after (sugar, spices, tobacco, coffee) and served as an outlet for the products of the mother country. We are indebted to Savary for a very clear explanation of the ideas, not only of Colbert, but of many of his contemporaries:

> It is certain that this commerce is more advantageous for the merchants, the public, and the State, than that which necessitates a long sea voyage, in that it transports over 4,000,000 *livres* worth of merchandise each year to all these countries. These are

commodities of this kingdom which are superflous at home because
of their too great abundance. The colonial commerce also results
in bringing merchandise amounting to over 6,000,000 *livres* back
to France—an operation which increases the revenue of the State
by the import duties. The goods are sold and distributed to the
public at half the price at which foreigners sold them before the
establishment of the West India Company (*Compagnie d'Occident*). . . . such goods do not harm any manufacturers of the
kingdom; and, what is worthy of serious thought, no money or
very little money is sent into those countries. In carrying on trade
in the North, on the Baltic, in Muscovy, and in the East Indies,
on the other hand, money must necessarily be used. Without it,
a trader could not be successful there.

The West Indian islands of France (San Domingo, Martinique, and Guadeloupe) developed rapidly in the second
half of the seventeenth century; and an important colonial
trade resulted. Wines, brandies, salt meats, codfish, herrings,
oil, cheese, iron, woolens, linens, and silk goods went out from
France; sugar, tobacco, coffee, and cotton came in return. The
slave trade also proved most lucrative. The colonial commerce soon enriched the merchants of Bordeaux, La Rochelle,
Rouen, Nantes, and even St.-Malo;[16] and they were led to
seek a monopoly of the trade with the American Islands for
themselves. In this they were not successful, for in spite of the
efforts of Colbert, the English and the Dutch were able to
circumvent the measures taken by the French government.
The English could ill spare the products of the French Antilles.[17] Furthermore—and there is no better proof of the
progress of commercial capitalism—the time had come when
commercial monopolies were threatened everywhere.

At the end of the seventeenth century, the Pacific market
began to attract French shipowners, and especially those of
St.-Malo. The latter sought to secure this very important outlet for the linens of Normandy and Brittany, the cloths and
silks of Lyons and Touraine, and a variety of other goods,

including laces, beaver hats, woolen and silk stockings, silk goods, cutlery and paper. Profits of at least 40 to 50 per cent were common in the trade. At this time men of affairs like Jourdan de Grouée, or shipowners like Noël Danycan, fitted out vessels to trade with the Pacific coast. In 1706, three boats belonging to Danycan brought profits of 350 per cent.

Considerable trade was also carried on with the Spanish colonies, although the treaty of Utrecht had granted the privilege of the slave trade to the English. French shipowners, especially the shipowners of St.-Malo, carried on a contraband trade with the Spanish colonies which brought in very fair profits for a number of years. Of this group was Magon de la Balue who maintained a most lucrative trade with the Spanish colonies,—a trade financed in part with funds which had been deposited with him, notably the funds of a president of the Dijon parliament. The gains from his shipping enterprises served to swell his capital. Nantes did not fall behind St.-Malo. By 1715, Nantes had an enormous trade with Guinea and with the American islands, and many of her shipowners had become very rich. Fifty years earlier (1664) the city had possessed only around 40 "two deckers" almost exclusively engaged in codfishing, and about 100 one-deck ships, which carried on the trade with Spain, England, and Holland.

The outstanding capitalists of the period were recruited from this shipowning class; and in the next century, they often participated with financiers in organizing and managing great industrial enterprises. Thus Noël Danycan, mentioned a moment ago, obtained control of the mines of Brittany and Bourbonnais.

IX. WEAKNESS OF THE FRENCH FINANCIAL ORGANIZATION

Very clearly capitalism made much slower progress in France than in Holland and England. The French experience with the corporate form of organizations affords further proof of this conclusion. French corporations were both less numerous and less strongly established than the similar business units of Holland and England. Such corporations as were founded in France during the second half of the seventeenth century were not the result of a natural development but of the efforts of a minister of state, Colbert. Is it surprising therefore that Jacques Savary should mainly recommend the formation of limited partnerships (*sociétés en commandite*) as a means whereby commercial enterprises could procure considerable capital? Companies with a collective name (*Sociétés on nom collectif*) also seem to have been established. In fact Savary declares:

> In places where there is a considerable manufacturing industry like Paris, Lyons, Saint-Chamond, Tours, Sedan, Amiens, Chalons, Rheims, Rouen, Laval and other cities of the kingdom, there are several associations of business men who carry on trade in the necessary raw materials. These they sell to the workmen, from whom in turn they buy the manufactured merchandise, which is later to be sold to people from other cities who buy on the spot, or else who retain them to make such purchases.

The weakness of the French banking system is further evidence of the relatively backward position of the country. Lyons alone was still an important capital market; and, while the operations of the Lyons banks seem to have facilitated relations with Italy, they occupied a relatively less important place than during the sixteenth century. Their business was not confined to exchange operations and money changing, however; they participated in the trade in precious metals, acted as intermediaries for payments, received deposits, and carried on a discounting business.

Settlements of accounts (*virements de partie*) were still carried on at Lyons, much as in the sixteenth century. The

Memoir of the Intendant d'Herbigny (1697) considers this practice quite minutely. It is clear that he is describing the germ of the modern clearing house:

> The first fifteen days after the opening of payments are used in making agreements between creditors and debtors, concerning the method of payment, that is to say, whether a note will be continued or whether it will be paid in writing or in cash. These agreements are either negotiated directly with each other or through exchange brokers who act as intermediaries. During the last fifteen days, payments are made in writings through *virements de partie*, or, in other words, by compensation. All of the merchants and others carrying balances assemble in the exchange room from ten o'clock in the morning until noon, and by the comparison of balances, seeing reciprocally their debtors and their creditors, they adjust so well the payments to be made to one another that sometimes only 100,000 crowns *(écus)* in cash are paid out, covering business transactions amounting to 20 millions.

Elsewhere in France, however, the banking organization was very defective. A direct remittance of funds was possible only to England. Transfers of funds to other countries involved turning to the Bank of Hamburg and especially to the Bank of Amsterdam, which held the undisputed supremacy in this business. This condition is one of the reasons why, as Professor Henri Hauser has remarked, French exchange was "a depreciated exchange" throughout the reign of Louis XIV. This statement throws great light on the economic condition of France in the seventeenth century.

At Lyons, the merchants and bankers had obtained the right to settle their affairs on 'change as early as the first half of the sixteenth century. From 1630 to 1653, the *bourse* was housed in a special building, and in the course of the seventeenth century several rulings, notably that of 1667, fixed the method of making payments, thus providing the model followed later by the London Clearing House. But *bourses* were few in France during the seventeenth century, and even the Paris *Bourse* did not yet exist.

X. FRENCH FINANCIERS AND THEIR OPERATIONS

Capitalism played a much less important rôle in France than in Holland or England; and the principal reason for this was the character of the part played by the French financiers. Their activities consisted mainly in profiting from the embarrassments of the Royal Treasury and in fattening themselves at its expense. This class of financiers was very numerous, including, as it did, the royal treasurers. One of Necker's first efforts in 1778 and 1779 aimed at cutting down the long list of such officials. In addition, there were the treasurers of the states, notably in Brittany and Languedoc, who acted as bankers for their provinces and also for the King. These bankers, like the Harouys and the Creissels, carried on financial operations on a large scale, though sometimes such operations resulted in spectacular bankruptcies.

Not less numerous were the tax collectors of all sorts: the general tax collector in every principal district; collectors of poll taxes at each election; collectors of the tithes, of the State payments, of the "general farm" (*ferme générale*), and of deposits (*consignations*). Paymasters for the government securities (*rentes*), each kind with its own special paying officer, were likewise numerous; and there were also the paymasters of the wages of the royal court.

Study of the records of a single town will show how numerous and how prosperous were the financial officers who resided in it. They fell in the group of inhabitants whose *capitation* tax was the highest. At Rennes, during the eighteenth century, for example, there were such officers as the agents of the royal domains, the collectors of the hearth tax, as it had long been called, the director of provisions (*directeur des*

vivres), the employees engaged in the collection of the tax
called the dues (*devoir*), and the officers of the mint. These
people all had very high tax quotas, and the collector for the
domains was taxed at 600 *livres*. The importance of such
financial officers (to whom the farmers-general should be
added), grew steadily; and they did not content themselves
with fulfilling their administrative functions. They entered
into business and traded with the funds of the government.

In a word, they became part of a group which was as rich
as it was execrated—a group which came to be called contractors (*traitants*) or *partisans*. By making advances to the
Royal Treasury, these obtained the right either to collect a
particular tax, or to distribute the numerous jobs of all sorts,
created by the royal government. Such was notably the case
in the latter years of the reign of Louis XIV.

Thus, these contractors (*traitants*) were engaged in a
special kind of business (*affaires extraordinaires*) upon which
the royal government must depend, since the old taxes no
longer sufficed for its needs. The profits which they realized
at the expense of the Treasury were enormous. Even in Colbert's time, the *traitants* retained 1,320,000 *livres* out of a
total of 14,420,000 *livres*, without counting any other profits;
in all they retained 2,333,000 *livres*, almost a sixth of the
total. According to Boulainvilliers, they received 266 millions
on contracts amounting to a billion between 1689 and 1709,
or a fourth of the total. They were able to do this because they
enforced demands which grew with the embarrassment of the
public Treasury. In 1694, after five years of war, Vauban
estimated that the *partisans* had obtained around 100 millions.

To be sure, it was quite impossible to carry on the government without the participation of persons possessing large
capital. Most of the bankers of the age—among whom may
be cited de Meuves, Hoggers, as well as Samuel Bernard him-

self—had much more to do with the public credit than with commerce. Moreover, it must be recognized that financiers, like Samuel Bernard, the Crozats, or even such as Le Gendre, rendered great services at the most critical moments of the War of the Spanish Succession. Several times Samuel Bernard ran the risk of complete ruin.

Furthermore, war contractors (*munitionnaires*) and war treasurers were more grasping than the bankers (if such be possible); and they often speculated on the outlook for famine. Was it not by carrying on a traffic in war supplies that the brothers Paris began to build up their fortune? They, indeed, were perhaps the greatest capitalists of the whole eighteenth century. On the other hand, numerous financiers were ruined in the course of their career, or suffered very cruelly. Sometimes also—though rarely—they were forced to make restitution (*rendre gorge*).[18] More numerous were those who founded noble families, like that Béchameil whose son, Béchamel de Nointel, became Ambassador to Constantinople and Intendant of Brittany.

To what extent did the capital accumulated by the financiers aid in the expansion of industrial and commercial capitalism? It is difficult to estimate this with anything like precision. Doubtless, some of the silent partners of the shipowners, like the Magons of St.-Malo, were drawn from their ranks; and they were among those who subscribed to the stock of the first great industrial enterprises, notably the companies engaged in mining metals or coal. Pâris-Duverney, for example, put a great deal of money in the development of the silver-lead mine at Pontpéan. In part, also, the newly and rapidly acquired wealth was used to acquire landed property or seigniories; and much was dissipated in supporting a life of leisure.

Much of the capital seems to have been in a way "immoblized," however, when its owners took up parliamentary employments—a costly luxury in the seventeenth century—or when they occupied one of the innumerable offices created by the royal power. Investments were made principally in government bonds (*rentes*), the amount of which multiplied ceaselessly after the sixteenth century. As early as 1589 there were 3,428,000 *livres* of such bonds. The royal government constantly created new debts and evaded payments by means of "reductions," a sort of repudiation upon terms that were ruinous to the holders of *rentes*. Occasionally, also, the quarterly interest payments were omitted. Colbert prided himself on the "reductions" he had engineered; in 1670 he had cut down the volume of bonds outstanding by one-third. But constant borrowings continued after his time; and promises were again broken at the expense of the unlucky bondholders. In 1789, there were 62 millions of perpetual *rentes* owed by the Royal Treasury; and those owed by the Church (which were much safer investments than those owed by the state) amounted to 149 millions. There were also *rentes* of the provincial governments such as those issued by the Estates of Brittany, for example; these bore the moderate rates of 4 and 5 per cent, because they offered ample security.

The preceding discussion supports the conclusion that the expansion of the financial operations of the government, the number of functionaires and government officers, and the volume of the government debt alike contributed to retard the expansion of industrial and commercial capitalism in France.

CHAPTER VI

THE EXPANSION OF COMMERCIAL AND FINANCIAL CAPITALISM IN THE EIGHTEENTH CENTURY

THE eighteenth century—at least, the first half of the century—does not mark a new period in the history of capitalism: commercial capitalism still continues supreme. The accumulations of capital are becoming so considerable, however, that the way is fast being prepared for further transformations.

I. THE ECONOMIC DECADENCE OF HOLLAND

In the course of the new century, England comes to hold first rank in the economic rivalry; Holland is relegated to second place. The decline in Holland's greatness, though slow at first, gained momentum steadily. It was not very clearly marked until after 1730 or even 1750, but the first symptoms of the decadence—the causes of which deserve the careful attention of historian and sociologist—are to be discovered in the first third of the eighteenth century.

No doubt, the wars of Louis XIV had already undermined Holland's great maritime power in some measure. But the essential causes lay deeper: Holland possessed only a restricted territory, her natural resources were neither abundant nor varied, and her industrial efforts contributed but feebly to the supply of goods for export. Moreover, the volume of manufactured goods tended to fall off during the eighteenth century because other countries which possessed resources in raw materials acted in the interest of their own manufacturers—

and took steps toward prohibiting the export of such materials to Holland. The Dutch trade thus tended to become almost exclusively a commission trade. This was extremely prosperous, to be sure; but in the end, the great powers with a variety of goods suitable for export, like England and France, were destined to outdistance Holland. At the close of the eighteenth century, therefore, England forged ahead in the struggle for commercial supremacy, even in the Baltic trade.

Amsterdam continued to hold her place as the great financial market of Europe, however, for Amsterdam possessed an enormous monetary stock and a powerful and well organized banking community. In this city, therefore, the bills of exchange and other "paper" of Europe were still negotiated, and all sorts of transferable securities were dealt in on the Amsterdam *Bourse*. By the second half of the eighteenth century, London begins to supplant Amsterdam, however, even in financial affairs.

II. THE MARITIME SUPREMACY AND COMMERCIAL EXPANSION OF ENGLAND

It is in the course of the eighteenth century, indeed, that the maritime and colonial supremacy of England is established. There is no need to dwell at length on the victorious struggle which she waged against France, both in America and India. From this point of view, the Treaty of Paris (1763) marks one of the most important dates of all history. England's triumph in America—which the War of Independence presently cut short—was much less far-reaching in its effects, however, than her seizure of India; for India was the gate to the Far East, and possession of India opened up a trade destined for a magnificent future.

English capitalism was stimulated by the growth of foreign trade during the course of the eighteenth century as well as by the expansion of the colonial empire. The outbound tonnage, which amounted to but 317,000 tons in 1700 and to 448,-000 tons in 1714, rose to 661,000 tons in 1751, to 959,000 tons in 1783, and, finally, to 1,958,000 tons in 1821.[1] The British foreign trade, amounting to seven and a half million pounds sterling in 1700, increased to 14 millions in 1801; and imports (which had amounted only to six million pounds sterling in 1715) rose to 16 millions in 1785, and to 30 millions in 1800. A further significant fact is that the curve for exports rose more rapidly than that for imports.[2]

It is clear also that capitalism in its commercial form continued to play the leading rôle during the eighteenth century. The export trade furnished the stimulus for the expansion of manufacturing industry. Were not those engaged in export trade the "exciters of industry" (*les excitateurs de l'industrie*), as Mantoux shows so vividly in his *Industrial Revolution?* Certainly there can be no doubt about the influence of the ports of Bristol, Yarmouth, and Hull upon the development of the cloth industry. The small manufacturers of cutlery at Birmingham, needing only a very simple equipment of tools, failed to bestir themselves very much; the stimulus toward large scale operations came from exporters. The latter undertook to give direction to the course of production. Such, for example, was Matthew Boulton of Soho, later the partner of Watt in the manufacture of the steam engine. The new cotton and silk industries, on the other hand, depended for their stimulus upon the importation of raw materials from the Far East.

Without doubt, it was the growth of the commercial centers which led to the development of the industrial centers. Before the seventeenth century, Liverpool had been a mere fishing village; during the eighteenth century, it gradually developed into a great seaport—one of the marvels of Great

Britain, as Defoe affirms. The tonnage entering the port increased from 27,000 tons in 1700 to 140,000 tons in 1770; and its population multiplied from 5,000 inhabitants in 1700 to over 34,000 in 1773. The expansion in the trade of Liverpool was due, especially, to its relations with the colonies and to the consequent importation of colonial wares, sugar, coffee, and cotton. The slave trade was also an important factor. But, like Nantes in France,[3] Liverpool served mainly as a transit market even before the development of the cotton industry in Lancashire had proceeded very far. Indeed, this industry owes its birth mainly to the progress of the great neighboring port; subsequently, the extension of the market comes to exercise a far-reaching influence on all economic activity.

The extraordinary importance of the English trade and commerce naturally attracted the attention of foreign observers, notably Voltaire who (in his *Tenth Philosophical Letter*) remarked pertinently:

> It is only because the English have become merchants and traders that London has surpassed Paris in extent and in the number of its citizens; that the English can place 200 warships on the sea and subsidize allies. . . . All this creates a just pride in an English merchant and makes it possible for him to compare himself, not without some right, to a Roman citizen.

The expansion of commercial activity by England explains, in large part, the importance attached by an economist like Adam Smith to the freedom of international trade, whereas agricultural questions held the first place in the philosophizing of the French Physiocrats. Adam Smith aimed his attack directly at the mercantilist doctrines. He attacked the belief that one nation can be enriched only at the expense of other countries, and he protested energetically against the old trade restrictions.[4]

III. FLOWERING OF FINANCIAL CAPITALISM IN ENGLAND

A natural consequence of the very remarkable expansion of the English maritime and colonial commerce was the flowering of financial capitalism. This is revealed by some very striking figures. The capital of the Bank of England had been fixed originally at 1,200,000 pounds sterling. In 1697, this was increased to 2,200,000 pounds and in 1710 to 5,559,000 pounds. So flourishing was the business of the Bank of Scotland that a 20 per cent dividend was distributed to its shareholders. A very grave crisis intervened in 1708, to be sure; but thirty corporations survived, and there was soon a new fever of speculation, such as had never before been experienced. A great number of companies were created to engage in mining, fishing, manufacturing and the building of port works,—without counting a variety of other more or less chimerical and even fraudulent enterprises.

Then occurred the famous episode of the South Sea Bubble. The South Sea Company was created in 1711, with a nominal capital of nine million pounds. In organization it resembled Law's *Compagnie d'Occident* closely; and like Law's enterprise it also was responsible for a mad speculation. Curiously enough this occurred at almost exactly the same time as did the speculation in France, that is to say, in 1719 to 1720. Between January and May 1720 the price of all classes of shares rose rapidly: shares of the Bank of England rose 36 per cent; those of the East India Company, 34 per cent; of the South Sea Company, 225 per cent; and shares of the African Company, 300 per cent. In May, South Sea shares sold for 600 pounds sterling and in June they sold for 1,050 pounds. This marked the peak of the inflation for this, as for the other companies; and, naturally, as the bubble burst, the boom ended in a rapid collapse. In September 1720 came the panic, in the course of which company shares fell disastrously.[5]

The South Sea Bubble has come to be symbolic of the whole variety of new corporations, and of all the booms and bubbles which were promoted at that moment. The consequences of the crash were severe; but they were less disastrous than those which followed Law's failure in France. In a few years, the English were again turning to those capitalistic enterprises which made it possible to undertake many new and fruitful branches of trade and commerce.[6] At this time, also, the founding of the stock exchange created machinery which had the effect of "regularizing" speculation in transferable securities.[7] Thus England, by the first third of the eighteenth century, was exhibiting all the characteristics of modern capitalism: the fever for speculation, manipulation on the stock exchange, and crisis succeeding a boom. These same phenomena (though perhaps on a smaller scale) had been experienced by Holland as early as the seventeenth century.

The creation of capitalistic insurance companies constitutes another significant development. Life insurance and fire insurance began about the same time.[8] Maritime insurance, of course, was not a new idea. It had existed since the Middle Ages in Italy; but not until the period of the South Sea Company in England did corporations begin to compete with individual insurers. Two such companies were formed: the London and the Royal Exchange Assurance Corporations. In 1706, the Company of London Insurers was formed to undertake the insurance of both houses and merchandise against fire; and in 1714 The Union or Double Hand in Hand Fire Office was founded. At this point also, the connection which exists between insurance and gambling or speculation should be noted. If insurance is a guaranty of security for the insured, the insurer, especially in maritime matters, necessarily assumes a risk, to use the word now current. Certainly the development of insurance is one of the phenomena which mark the progress of capitalism.

Thus, we see how and why financial capitalism in England grew in strength and power. And soon Amsterdam was no longer the only place possessed of an enormous monetary stock. After the treaty of Methuen in 1703, England received a great deal of Brazilian gold from Portugal and built up great reserves of the precious metals from this source.[9] In the second half century, therefore, she gained upon Amsterdam as the center of international finance. The English banking organization was not as well developed as that of Holland, however; there were but few country banks until toward the end of the eighteenth century, although many merchants carried on banking operations in addition to their principal business. In the beginning, therefore, the absence of banking facilities was a handicap to the development of large scale industry (*la grande industrie*) in England.

IV. THE SLOWER AND LESS INTENSE PROGRESS OF CAPITALISM IN FRANCE

Capitalism developed much more slowly in France than in England, even during the eighteenth century. The reason for this is readily understood: for the foreign trade of France, especially her maritime and colonial commerce, was much less flourishing than that of England. The trade with Spain, especially that with Cadiz, was still considerable, though it tended to fall off during the second half of the eighteenth century; and the commerce with Holland was less important than it had been during the seventeenth century. The trade with England was still hampered by customs duties which would have been almost prohibitive, except for the smuggling operations.

On the other hand, trade with Italy and Germany expanded appreciably, as did that with the countries of the North, although this latter trade was still carried on through Dutch intermediaries. The commerce with the Levant was still flourishing (whatever some may have claimed to the contrary), since French imports from the Levant amounted to 36 million *livres* on the eve of the Revolution, and exports to 28 millions.

With France, as with England, colonial trade held first place in the eighteenth century. The East India Company (*Compagnie des Indes*), reëstablished in 1723 after the fall of Law, continued to carry on a considerable trade with India and Japan. In the period 1743–1756, its profits amounted to some 72 million *livres* a year; but soon it was dealt mortal blows, first by the Seven Years' War and then by the Treaty of Paris. In 1768, profits fell to 18 million *livres*, and in 1769 the Company ceased to exist.[10] The loss of Canada, then but little developed or exploited, was much less severely felt than the loss of the Indian posts.

Nor did French trade with the Antilles (any more than the peopling of these islands) cease to expand during the eighteenth century. The West Indian trade was very flourishing at the eve of the Revolution, and the French consumption of colonial products (sugar, coffee, tobacco, and, in the second half of the century, cotton) had increased very appreciably. The trade with the Antilles, only some 26 million *livres* in 1716, reached 260 millions in 1788, a very considerable figure for the period. Two thousand ships were engaged in the slave trade alone. The importance of the colonial trade explains the great prosperity of such Atlantic ports as Bordeaux and Nantes, as well as the very marked progress of Le Havre. The merchants and shipowners of Marseilles were no longer concerned with trade in the Mediterranean alone, and their operations took on a world importance. Indeed, the foreign trade of France quadrupled between 1715 and 1789—a very rapid

rate of progress, a rate relatively more rapid, indeed, than that
of English commerce. In 1788, its value exceeded a billion
livres. These facts indicate that the capital accumulation
which foretells the dawning of an industrial revolution came
mainly from the maritime and colonial commerce. Even in
the course of the eighteenth century, the cotton manufacturing industry around Rouen was stimulated by the import trade
in cotton through the ports of Normandy; and at Nantes, the
trade with the "islands of America" had given rise to sugar
refining and the manufacture of calico.

V. FINANCIAL CAPITALISM IN FRANCE

Financial capitalism in France, like commercial capitalism,
had far less scope for its operations than in England. Law's
scheme, to be sure, had promoted a fever of speculation there
similar to that which raged during the South Sea speculation
in England. There was an excessive rise in the price of the
shares of his *Société* (exceeding 900 per cent), and there was
an appalling inflation of the currency. According to the report of Bourgeois, the cashier, Law's bank issued notes
amounting to over 3 billions of *livres*. As a consequence of this
inflation, prices rose more than 100 per cent, a fact which
impressed itself upon all observers.[11] Certainly Law's downfall and the collapse of his "system" had the effect of retard-
ing the progress of credit in France; for a long time people
had little confidence in "paper" and securities. Nevertheless,
even the activities of Law seem to have been beneficial in
some particulars. Thus, as Gaston Martin has shown in his
study of the port of Nantes, it apparently stimulated commercial expansion.

Meanwhile, the banking business—the history of which is
still but little known—continued to grow. In Paris, there was
an appreciable increase in the number of bankers; and in 1721

Mre JEAN LAW CON^{er} DU ROY EN TOUS CES CON^{its} CONTROLEUR GNÀL DES FINANCES en 1720.

Sous l'Auguste et Sage Regence LAW consommé dans l'art de regir la finance
D'un Prince aimant la bonne foy Trouve l'art d'enrichir les sujets et le Roy

there were 51 such, whereas there had been only 21 in 1703. While the Parisian bankers concerned themselves particularly with the public credit, they also did business with the great merchants and traders (*négociants*).[12] The banking houses of Marseilles, despite the slight capitals at their disposal, specialized in commercial operations with the Levant; while at Bordeaux and Rouen, the banks did business mainly with the shipowners. After the downfall of Law, the Bank of Lyons no longer held the prominent place it had attained during the sixteenth and, to a lesser degree, in the seventeenth century. In these various French banks, or at least in the Parisian banks, a prominent place was held by natives of Geneva, such as the Thélussons.[13] In general, however, banking had not yet become the principal occupation of a body of strictly specialized men of business; instead it was an accessory occupation undertaken both by merchants and traders (*négociants*), and also by numbers of public financiers (*gens de finance*) such as the farmers-general, the receivers-general, and the receivers for the states.

In 1776 a credit institution of broad powers, the *Caisse d'Escompte*, was created. This was a joint stock company with a capital of 15 million *livres*, increased later to 100 millions. Its essential function was that of discounting commercial bills; and here it rendered valuable service to commerce and industry. Its existence was threatened during Necker's second ministry, on the eve of the Revolution, however, when it was obliged to make loans to the royal treasury in volume and on terms. But its establishment was, none the less, a significant index of the progress of capitalism in France.

In the eighteenth century, also, the Paris *Bourse* was founded (1724). It was placed under the jurisdiction of the lieutenant-general of Paris. From ten in the morning to one in the afternoon, on every day except Sundays and holidays, men of business (*négociants*), merchants, bankers, financiers, exchange and merchandise brokers (*agents de change et de commerce*) assembled. The regulations required that all bills of exchange and all notes payable to bearer or to order should be negotiated at the *Bourse*. Business concerning transfers of merchandise and negotiable paper was likewise to be transacted at the *Bourse:* and, when papers or bills having to do with a commercial transaction were to change hands, the employment of an exchange agent or broker as intermediary was obligatory.[14] The establishment of the Paris *Bourse* facilitated all sorts of transactions; but in the eighteenth century its activities were by no means comparable with those of the Amsterdam *Bourse*. It should be noted, finally, that financial transactions were more important at Paris than commercial transactions.

In the eighteenth century, also, the first great insurance corporation was created in France, though not until the middle of the century. In 1750, the Maritime Insurance Company (*Compagnie d'assurances maritimes*) was founded; and in 1753 this was transformed into the General Insurance Company (*Compagnie d'assurances générales*) which undertook also to insure houses against loss by fire. The capital had been fixed at 4,500,00 *livres* in 1750; but this was increased to 12,-000,000 *livres* the following year. Shares were 3,000 *livres* each. The insurance premiums charged by the company were very moderate for those days; and its competition proved dangerous for those private insurers who were so numerous in the seaports. But in insurance matters, France again found herself trailing behind those powers which were more active economically.[15]

It is interesting to note also that the first fire insurance company did not insure furniture, while the second, which was created November 6, 1786—under the title of *Compagnie d'assurances contre l'incendie* (Fire Insurance Company)—insured furniture but not jewels or securities. Life insurance developed quite late; it was not until November 3, 1789, that the right to engage in that business was conferred on the *Compagnie d'assurances contre l'incendie* for a period of fifteen years. Actually that company did not function beyond 1793.[16] Presently, however, the Committee on Poverty of the Assembly (*le Comité de mendicité de la Constituante*) took up the creation of a scheme for social insurance. Inspiration for this came from the mathematician, Duvillard, whose *Researches Covering* Rentes, *Loans and Repayments*, published in 1787, received the approval of the Academy of Sciences.

To understand exactly the extent of capitalism in the eighteenth century, it is not enough to consider Paris alone, nor the great industrial and commercial centers. In the towns of secondary importance, little capital had yet been accumulated, nor was money in general circulation. Thus, Yves-Fr. Besnard says in his *Recollections of a Nonagenarian:* "Not a single banker was then known (around 1770) at Angers, nor a single millionaire, in trade or even in the nobility." The largest dowries were not over twenty thousand *livres*. Those of ten thousand made a stir. And he adds, "Men gladly retired from business when they possessed an income of three or four thousand *livres*, a sum then considered, throughout the Third Estate, as a very respectable fortune." In the small towns, the villages, and the country, capital was still scarce; and this lack of capital is one of the reasons explaining the backward condition of agriculture.

VI. SOMBART'S THEORY

Why did capitalism in both its commercial and financial forms develop so much more fully in Holland and in England than in France? Sombart answers this question by saying that the credit belongs to the Jews. The latter had become firmly established in Holland before the end of the sixteenth century and in England during the course of the seventeenth century. Still other historians, like Weber and Troeltsch, think that it was the Calvinists and the Puritans who played the decisive rôle. But can phenomena of such broad implications be attributed to a single cause? Doubtless, the Jews did occupy a very important place, especially in the overseas trade of the seventeenth and eighteenth centuries.[17] But was not Holland a great maritime power before the settlement of the Jews at Amsterdam in 1593? And as early as the beginning of the seventeenth century,—well before the influx of Jewish men of affairs,—had not capitalism attained a vigor which pointed to the future destiny of England?[18]

Yet the theses of Sombart, Weber and Troeltsch do seem to contain a share of truth; for the Jews and the Puritans alike were able to contribute—though in what measure, it is impossible to say exactly—to the bringing into play of a "capitalistic mentality" in the countries mentioned. In contrast with the Catholics (and even the Lutherans), neither the Jews nor the Puritans placed the spiritual above the temporal. They held the acquisition of wealth to be a praiseworthy occupation and advocated a simple mode of life in order to save and to accumulate capital. The influence which both exercised on the evolution of capitalism is to be explained in these terms.

During the eighteenth century, the merchants in French towns reproached the Jews for selling various articles at unduly low prices. It was pretended that such goods must be of inferior quality. As a result of this agitation the Jews were expelled from a number of localities, especially in the decade 1730–40. But they retained the right to sell at fairs; and since they were more active, more enterprising, and above all more hardworking, they often outdistanced their Christian competitors. Despite their precarious situation, therefore, some of them (like the Dalpugets of Bordeaux) were able to set up actual branches in a number of scattered towns. This method of organization was presently to prove very fruitful and to prosper during the following century.[19]

VII. THE MOBILIZATION OF ECONOMIC LIFE: SPECULATION AND PUBLICITY

But while the cause to which Professor Sombart attributes the triumph of capitalism appears inadequate, he has, none the less, described very forcefully what he calls the "commercialization" of economic life, or more accurately, the process of its "mobilization." This process went forward with great rapidity in the course of the eighteenth century. Professor Sombart shows that economic relations tended to become "impersonal," with the development of paper securities, including endorsed bills of exchange payable to bearer, shares and bonds (floated by commercial and industrial companies or by governments), and, finally, with the growth in the use of bank notes. A very interesting matter of business which he has brought to light is the creation, in the eighteenth century, of a mortgage credit (*crédit hypothécaire*) for the benefit of the Dutch colonists of Surinam. Their plantations constituted the security for the sums borrowed of the mortgage banks.

Sombart has also demonstrated the great progress of security speculation on the exchanges of Amsterdam, Hamburg, and London during the eighteenth century. Such progress was related to the expansion of commercial affairs, moreover; and, on this account, it was not until well toward the end of the *Ancien Régime* that speculation in securities became active at Paris. Then it attained such proportions as to occasion the Decrees of Council dated August 7 and October 2, 1785, and confirmed by the decree of September 21, 1786, which declared "void the dealings in and pledging of royal notes or any others payable in the future, without delivery of the said notes or without their actual deposit"; though the later decree alluded to dealings of which it is very difficult to discover the thread of the negotiations.[20]

During the greater part of the eighteenth century, however, future speculation in the funds was frowned upon, even in capitalistic circles. In the British House of Commons in 1773, a violent attack was made against the infamous practices of stockjobbing (*l'agiotage en Bourse*). To the author of the *Universal Dictionary of Trade and Commerce*, Malachy Postlethwayt, these stockjobbing operations were a veritable public scandal;[21] and both David Hume and Adam Smith used terms quite as vigorous when denouncing speculation in the exchanges. The *Treatise on Credit* (*Traité du crédit et de la circulation*) of Joseph de Pinto (published in 1771) was unique at this time in describing the trade in securities and the speculation in the funds, both with great precision and with praise.

Another sign that the eighteenth century constitutes a new era is the birth and progress of advertising. Professor Sombart has also shown very forcibly the extent to which resort to advertising ran counter to old economic customs. The aim of the guilds had been to ensure a means of livelihood for all the masters, notably by procuring the necessary labor force for them. The idea of competition ran counter to the thought of the craftsmen and merchants of the time. The master was quietly to await customers in his shop; and such was even the situation presented in Defoe's *Complete English Tradesman* at the beginning of the eighteenth century. Under such circumstances, the use of commercial notices and advertisements appeared as a disloyal competitive proceeding. Commercial announcements began to appear in Holland during the last third of the seventeenth century, however, and in England at the end of that century. The history of advertising, and especially the history of its origins, has been only roughly sketched thus far and deserves exact research.

Here again, France was backward; the *Dictionnaire de Commerce* of Savary des Brulons defined the word *réclame* as a printing term and *affiche* still conveyed the general meaning of "placard." Not until 1751 were the weekly papers called the *Petites Affiches* founded in Paris, an example soon followed in many provincial towns;[22] and commercial advertisements multiplied but slowly even in these. An ordinance of 1761 still designated it a reprehensible practice for the merchants of Paris to distribute notices to the public announcing the sale of merchandise at prices lower than usual. Therefore advertising failed to make real progress in France until the years preceding the Revolution, or, in other words, until the very moment when great economic activity had become manifest.

In a word, these new financial and commercial practices indicate the approaching triumph of capitalism in all its forms.

VIII. THE RISE OF PRICES

Is not the rise of prices during the eighteenth century and especially during the second half of that century related to the expansion of capitalism? In the main, this rise affected agricultural products (wheat, meat, eggs, etc.), farm rents (which sometimes increased by 100 per cent) and, consequently, the price of land. Since the technical improvements resulting from the industrial progress were resulting in a slight decline of the prices of manufactured articles, Arthur Young, in his *Travels in France*, attributed this rise of agricultural prices to an increase in population. But was it not mainly the result of an increase of capital such as generally leads to a fall in the value of money? This difficult question has not yet been studied with adequate scientific care; and for the moment it is possible only to formulate hypotheses. In any case, however, a phenomenon is disclosed which is analagous to the rise of prices in the sixteenth century, though on a smaller scale.

CHAPTER VII

THE PROGRESS OF CAPITALISM AND THE BREAK-DOWN OF THE COLONIAL SYSTEM

I. THE COLONIAL SYSTEM OF SPAIN DURING THE EIGHTEENTH CENTURY

THE breakdown of the colonial system is one of the most significant evidences of progress in the evolution of modern capitalism. This breakdown is clearly seen in the Spanish experience of the eighteenth century; for the absurd system regulating the trade with the Spanish colonies in America naturally led to an increase of illicit trade and smuggling. The benefits to the mother country from that trade therefore dropped off steadily and even threatened to disappear.

Foreigners, and especially the French, protested against the regulations by which the trade of Cadiz was controlled; and even this trade became more precarious and more irregular. French policy between 1715 and 1725 also seems to have had a particularly bad effect on French commercial interests in Spain; and suspension of the sailings of the galleons and of the fleets in 1735, and the substitution of certain privately owned boats which were granted permission to carry on that trade (*registros*), aggravated rather than helped the situation. In 1755, therefore, everyone was glad to see the fleets re-established. The dissatisfaction did not end, however; and Charles III was compelled to give way to a certain extent and to recognize the principle of "freedom of trade," for his order of 1778 (*ordenanza del comercio libre*) suppressed the monopoly held by Cadiz. On the other hand, Charles did his best to protect Spanish industry from foreign competition, mostly by using prohibitive tariffs. Certainly it would be unfair not to recognize that the Spanish government did its best to foster the development of colonial trade, especially in the second half of the eighteenth century. Then, too, the great economic progress of the Spanish colonies, especially in the Argentine, must be taken into account. A significant development pointing to this progress was the creation of the viceroyalty of Buenos Aires, set apart from Peru in 1777. It was already becoming difficult to fetter intercolonial trade, and the time was not far away when the Spanish colonies in America would set up their claim to independence, mainly for economic reasons.

But other maritime powers than Spain were able to profit from the trade with Spanish and Portuguese America, as has already been noted. Both England and Holland were successful in carrying on an illicit trade and so also, though to a lesser yet not inconsiderable extent, was France. England pushed to the forefront during the eighteenth century, both because her control of Portugal (insured by the treaty of Methuen in 1703) placed Brazilian gold in her hands,[1] and because the development of British industries provided her with a more favorable basis of trade than was possessed by any other nation.

Furthermore, overseas commerce had attained relatively large proportions, especially the trade with America—both legal and illicit; and this development of maritime trade was the basis of a great accumulation of capital by the powers bordering the Atlantic. At this very time, manufacturing was making rapid strides in England and also, though to a lesser extent, in France. The inflowing stream of specie and of the precious metals became very great in the second half of the seventeenth and during the eighteenth century, and the development of the Spanish colonies steadily increased their demands for the manufactured goods of Europe.. Nor can the enormous profits of smuggling be left out of account, or those accruing from an illicit trade which, as it was carried on, could hardly be distinguished from piracy. Like the operations of the English privateers, it might even be called common robbery. Thus, robbery (*Raub*), to use Sombart's phrase, seems to have been one of the sources of modern capitalism.

II. THE COLONIAL SYSTEM OF ENGLAND IN NORTH AMERICA

The problem of commercial monopoly presently comes up for solution, even in England. The English colonies in North America date from the beginning of the seventeenth century. What shall be the relationship between the mother country and the colonies? Will not the economic development of the New World create a clamor for independence on the part of the English colonies? Will not this agitation develop even though the English colonial system is obviously more reasonable, more flexible and less rigorous than the Spanish system?

From the first, the English colonists of North America enjoyed much less prosperity than the Spanish colonists of South America. The British adventurers of the sixteenth century came to the New World looking for precious metals, tropical products, and especially for the famous passage that was to open the way to India. In great part these hopes were blasted. Still, Virginia, the first region to be colonized, possessed certain resources; and soon a new type of colony was created, the resident colony (*peuplement*) in the modern sense of the word. In New England, with its more severe climate, the founding of the permanent settlements became a marked characteristic of the colonies. The Crown and the Companies were especially interested in establishing numerous settlements, since success in this direction would increase the value of land. As a consequence, the English colonies of North America were not subjected to purely mercantilist regulations. Moreover, they were in part inhabited by refugees, including in their ranks many political and religious dissenters, who aspired to be more or less independent of the mother country.

But here it is that capitalism, at least commercial capitalism, made rapid progress during the first half of the seventeenth century, and especially toward the middle of the century. This fact explains the triumph of the mercantile system in the English colonial policy. Emphasis upon the balance of trade, the regulation of imports and exports, the monopoly of trade reserved to the traders of the mother country—such are the essential principles of that system. With reference to the colonies, Malachy Postlethwayt in his *Great Britain's Commercial Interest Explained and Improved*, first published at London in 1747 (a second edition appearing in 1759), showed the true characteristics of the monopoly control sought by the mother country:

> Colonies ought never to forget what they owe to their mother country in return for the prosperity and riches they enjoy. Their gratitude, in that respect, and the duty they owe indispensably oblige them to be immediately dependent on their original parent and to make their interest subservient thereunto. The effect of that interest and of that dependency will be, to procure the mother country: (1) a greater consumption of the productions of her lands; (2) occupation for a greater number of the manufacturers, artisans, fishermen and seamen; (3) a greater quanity of such commodities as she wants.[2]

Such rules meant, of course, that the colonists must neither manufacture goods nor engage in cultivation, whenever the products of their efforts would compete with those of the mother country. Neither must they consume foreign goods or buy merchandise from foreign countries if their needs could be supplied from the mother country. The colonists were to engage in agriculture, but the transportation of their crops was to be reserved for English sailors. It was thought, as a matter of fact, that this régime would be quite as advantageous to the colonists as to England herself.

III. THE COMMERCIAL POLICY OF ENGLAND

The commercial and colonial policies of England, since based upon the principles just discussed, are readily understood therefore. As early as 1621, a royal decree had forbidden Virginia to export its products to foreign lands without first unloading them in England, though, to be sure, the activities of the Dutch rendered this regulation ineffective. The latter carried home a part of the Virginia tobacco which they received in exchange for European goods transported to the New World.

Still more important and more general in its scope was the Navigation Act of 1651. The principal provisions of that Act required: first, that merchandise coming from Asia, Africa or America be carried to England only on vessels of British registry, manned by crews the majority of which were English; and secondly, that merchandise coming from Europe be carried to England or her dependencies only on English vessels or on vessels belonging to the producing country.

The Act of 1660 was even stricter, since it directed that all transportation service between England and her colonies must be performed by English vessels belonging to Englishmen, Irishmen or English colonists, and that three-quarters of the members of the crew of such ships must be British. This regulation was designed to keep foreigners away from the colonies. It bore heavily on Virginia and Maryland, which

could make little progress without Dutch trade; but conditions in New England were improved since its only effect
was to stimulate the development of shipbuilding. The Act
of 1660 also enumerated a certain number of colonial products which could be transported only to England or to English colonies. The list of enumerated articles included sugar,
ginger, tobacco, cotton, indigo, and dye-wood; it was enlarged in 1706 and 1722 to include molasses, rice, materials
for shipbuilding, copper, and furs. Meanwhile, the Act of
1663 had required that no European merchandise could be
shipped to the colonies without passing through England.

For a considerable interval, however, the Navigation Acts
did not interfere greatly with the English colonists. It was to
Virginia's interest to sell its tobacco to England; and most of
the New England trade was naturally with the West Indies.
Moreover, the colonies were too far away and too large—
and their economic life was too independent of that of the
mother country—for the mercantilist system to be effectively
enforced; and from the first the colonists possessed a large
measure of self-government. Thus, conditions were such that
an illicit trade and smuggling operations could develop, despite the English laws. These, in fact, could affect the colonists' interests but very little.

During the last forty years of the century (1660–1700),
the mother country had very slight influence on the economic
life of the American colonies. They developed rather slowly
and their total population hardly exceeded 250,000 to 300,-
000 inhabitants, for the most part English, except in New
York where the Dutch were in the majority, and in Pennsylvania where numerous Dutch, Germans, and Swedes had settled. Necessarily agriculture was the principal economic activity, though the fur trade was important.

New England was a country of small farms, cultivated by
their owners; in the Middle Colonies were farms of moderate

size, often rented by their owners; and in the South were large rice and tobacco plantations. In New England some manufacturing began to develop: thus many ships were built in Massachusetts at a lesser cost than in England. Presently two-thirds of the merchant fleet of the mother country came from New England. The making of rum from molasses brought from the sugar islands of the West Indies also developed into an important industry there.

But shipping and trading were the principal resources of New England; to the mother country were sent fish, forest products, rum, and ships, though the Corn Laws prevented the sending of wheat. At the same time the West Indian trade (i. e., the trade with the Antilles) was expanding steadily. The molasses which New England required for the manufacture of rum came from the sugar islands; and the New England ships carried cereals, building lumber, and also negroes to the islands in exchange. Newport, Rhode Island, became a great center of the trade in slaves ("black ivory"). The commerce of New York, though on a smaller scale, was generally similar to that of New England. The total trade of the colonies was from one and one-half to two times as large as their trade with the mother country. In 1700, this amounted to 344,000 pounds sterling for exports and 395,000 pounds sterling for imports.

The outcome of the Revolution of 1688 proved extremely favorable to New England, as it meant freedom from the annoying policies of the Restoration. Therefore it seems clear that, at the end of the seventeenth century, the commercial monopoly of the mother country was not fully effective in spite of all the navigation and trade acts.

IV. ECONOMIC CAUSES OF THE WAR OF INDEPENDENCE

The progress of the British colonies of North America in the eighteenth century was undoubtedly due to their own efforts, and not to any aid from the mother country. Even as late as 1760, the population was only 1,600,000. Agriculture continued to play a considerable part in the economic life of the time, especially in the Middle Colonies which were engaged in producing cereals. In the South where tobacco, rice, and indigo were cultivated, the prosperity increased greatly. Indigo was introduced into South Carolina in 1741.

Manufacturing was still of secondary importance. In a small degree, this was the consequence of the colonial system, but in small degree only. The mother country, seeking to hold the American markets for its manufactured products, enacted laws to prevent the creation of a colonial industry, making cloth, hats, or steel. Assistance from the colonial governments did result in the creation of some manufacturing industry; but the lack of capital proved a great obstacle. In the eighteenth century, commercial enterprise was much more profitable in the New World; and consequently it attracted capital and the energies of men. The high rate of interest, 6 or 8 per cent, was unfavorable to the development of manufacturing; and the shortage of money had the same effect. An equally important handicap was the shortage of labor. Immigrants were steadily attracted to other and more profitable fields of activity. For this reason, attempts to develop an iron industry in the colonies failed. An interesting fact is that wages were higher than in Europe; in the textile trade, for instance, they were 50 per cent higher than in England.

Throughout the colonies, manufacturing establishments were small and widely scattered. In the latter half of the century, however, a slight tendency toward concentration was apparent; and small centers of manufacturing activity developed at Germantown, Lancaster, and Bethlehem in Pennsylvania and at Haverhill in Massachusetts. In 1750, a plant to manufacture cloth was started at Boston; and after 1760, and especially after 1770, the tendency toward localization made some progress in the textile trade. In 1775, the *United Company of Philadelphia for Promoting American Manufactures* was formed at Philadelphia. Jennies were introduced there and at Beverly; but the textile industry of the colonies was backward as compared with that of England, which had forbidden the exportation of machinery to America.[3] Plainly, however, the tardy industrial development of the British colonies was due less to the mercantile system than to the general conditions governing their economic evolution. Consequently, trade, rather than industry, was the field which attracted the efforts of the British colonists. Their trade multiplied enormously between 1700 and 1774—ten times, according to Burke.

The mother country attempted to derive the greatest possible benefit from this trade, and to reserve it to herself as much as possible. In this she was not successful, inasmuch as 40 per cent of the colonial import trade and 45 per cent of the export trade was done with countries other than England —notably with the West Indies, Nova Scotia, Newfoundland, Europe and Asia.

The following table presenting data for the year 1769 is quite significant:

Trade of the North American Colonies, 1769 (Pounds Sterling)

	Great Britain	Southern Europe	West Indies	Africa	Total
Imports	1,604,000	76,000	789,000	151,000	2,623,000
Exports	1,531,000	552,000	747,000	20,278	2,285,000

This table brings out clearly the great importance of the West Indian trade, a considerable element in which was the trade with the French islands which were sources of cheaper sugar and molasses. This competition from the French Islands explains why planters of the English sugar islands besought Parliament to pass the Sugar Act of 1733. This established

duties of 9 pence per gallon on rum, 6 pence per gallon on molasses, and 5 shillings per 100 pounds of sugar imported into
the colonies of the mainland.

Had that Act been rigidly enforced it would have injured
the colonies greatly; but it was in fact a dead letter from the
beginning, and no attention was paid to its provisions. Trade
with the French islands kept on as in the past; and not even
the Seven Years' War caused an interruption. Neutral ports
in the Dutch or Spanish islands were used as bases in the
trade; in 1759, for example, Monte Cristi, a Spanish port of
the northern coast of San Domingo, was visited by more than
one hundred vessels from North America.

The Sugar Act of 1764 was designed to be more effective.
It forbade the importation of rum from foreign colonies,
raised the duty on sugar from 5 shillings to 1 pound 7 shillings, but reduced that on molasses from 6 pence to 3 pence
per gallon. Two years later, the duty on molasses was reduced
to 1 penny, regardless of the place of origin. But the smuggling kept up and even this Sugar Act proved quite ineffective.

The importance of the trade with the sugar islands of the
West Indies was due to the close connection of that trade with
the trade in slaves; for the distillers of New England, in
order to secure the means for purchasing molasses, found the
slave trade profitable. The *asiento* permitted the transportation of 15,000 negroes yearly between 1713 and 1733, two-
thirds of whom went to the English colonies. As a consequence,
the number of negroes in those colonies increased very rapidly;
from 59,000 in 1714 to 195,000 in 1754 and to 697,000 in
1790.

The West Indian trade in salt provisions was also important
for New England, since it provided an outlet for the very
important fishing industry, in competition with the French.
Three hundred and sixty vessels (33,000 tons burden)—of

which 300 belonged to Massachusetts owners—were engaged in the cod fisheries.

Yet the conflict between the mother country and her colonies was destined to be more and more sharply drawn. On both sides the old tendencies were exaggerated. The mother country, influenced by conservatism and acting in part because of selfish interests, sought to ensure the economic dependence of the colonies. On the other hand, the principle of economic liberty, which was everywhere becoming popular, fortified the claims of the colonists.

Grenville, the English minister, was not satisfied with increasing the number of "enumerated articles" which could not be exported except to England; in 1766, therefore, he decided that all goods originating in the colonies must be shipped to England. Presently, the mother country attempted to establish a system of taxation. This action at once raised the question of the power of Parliament over the colonies and made the subordination of the colonies an acute political issue. The Stamp Act of 1765 first aroused opposition in the colonies; then in 1767 came the Townshend Acts imposing import duties on paper, glass, lead, and tea.

These miscellaneous measures at once brought up a question of principle: the colonists asserted that they were unwilling to pay the new duties, inasmuch as they were not represented in the British Parliament. Taxation without representation was the issue raised; and this issue, rather than the question of commercial liberty, played the important rôle during the exciting events which gave birth to the American Revolution. There was also a deep-seated difference in attitude of mind between the American colonists and the governing class in the mother country. The former had established truly democratic institutions in the New World, whereas the British aristocracy—quite content with a state of affairs which worked so advantageously for its interests—looked upon those who sought a change of régime as rebels.[4] It seems true, none the less, that unwise commercial legislation was an important underlying cause of the Revolution. The more prosperous trade grew to be, the more irritating and unbearable did any new attempts at interference or regulation by the mother country become. Thus the colonies needed complete independence for their future economic development.[5]

V. THE RELAXING OF CONTROL IN FRANCE

Each of the important maritime powers faced the same problems of colonial control and administration; but the character of the solutions worked out to meet those problems necessarily varied, as the colonial empires themselves varied in population and resources.

The population of the Spanish colonies, for example, consisted mainly of government officials (leaving out of account the slaves and those in but little better position) and of noble land owners who possessed immense estates. The Spanish colonists therefore sought only the right to establish commercial relations with foreigners; and they neither made a show of great feeling nor engaged in active agitation. The illicit trade satisfied their needs very largely. The English colonists of North America, on the other hand, were farmers, manufacturers, or traders; and as such they felt the direct need to escape from the monopoly control of the mother country. Possessed of free governments and enjoying a large degree of autonomy, they were determined to secure economic, political and religious independence. Even the necessity of fighting did not deter them from defending what they considered to be their rights. This is the reason why the Americans were the first to free themselves from the mother country. Through the

War of Independence, the North American colonies became a new nation, the United States of America.

The French colonists in the West Indies—though less independent than the British—were, however, less complacent than the Spanish creoles. With a great show of energy, they asserted their claim to the right to trade freely with foreigners. Their sugar and molasses could be sold to the English colonies of North America to best advantage, while on their own account, they had need for the lumber, flour, and fish which could be bought cheaper on the neighboring continent than in France. These considerations explain the failure of Colbert's commercial policy in the West Indies.

The loss of Canada and Louisiana stiffened the claims of the French islanders to a right to carry on the North American trade, and smuggling was resorted to, in order to get around the obstacles created by the existing legislation. Gradually, therefore, the government was forced to give in: after 1763, Choiseul authorized the British (by paying a duty of 8 *livres* per quintal) to import cod into the French islands, despite the clamor raised by French shipowners. Later came the decision of the Council of 1784 which allowed foreign ships to load in several ports of the French colonies, much to the discontent of the shipowners of the mother country, who had found a source of great wealth in the trade with American islands.

Thus it appears that the colonists of both Americas were unanimous in opposing the old colonial system, while the traders in each country of the Old World did their best to break down any monopoly favoring their rivals. At the same time they sought to retain any monopoly grants which worked in their own favor. Because of this conflict, the English and Spanish colonies rebelled; and the New World gave birth to young republics full of promise for the future.

This was the great event—one of the most important of all history—which had been in preparation for a century and a half. That it would occur had been determined by the economic evolution of civilized peoples, by the progress of that commercial capitalism which, once created by the great overseas trade, had gained steadily in strength. Capitalism in its commercial form led to the attempts to establish a colonial system which would operate in the interest of the mother country, a system which all the maritime powers sought to put into effect with more or less severity after the sixteenth century. Each was desirous of obtaining the products of the tropics and especially those precious metals which were considered the very source of wealth.

And, indeed, the inflow of precious metals, and the increase in the monetary stock has had tremendous influence on modern capitalism. This explains the world-wide importance attached to places like Cadiz where gold and silver arrived from the New World, or like Amsterdam which became the principal bullion market during the seventeenth century, or later London which succeeded to the place of Amsterdam in the second half of the eighteenth century.

In time, the old system was recognized as an obstacle to economic expansion; and the growth of capitalism fostered by the expanding colonial trade tended to break down the regulatory system. The attempted monopoly control in the interest of the mother country could not be maintained. Spain, where efforts to establish the mercantile system were pushed to the extreme, paid for its blindness by ruin. England left more freedom to her colonies and suffered less from the effort to establish such control; but even England had to abandon the attempt. The loss of the French Indies, which had been a principal factor in French maritime commerce during the eighteenth century, was due only indirectly to the colonial system, though, to be sure, the wars of the revolutionary era

arose in part from the maritime and colonial rivalry between
France and England which had existed for a century.

VI. THE UNDERLYING CAUSES OF THE COLONIAL
REVOLUTIONS

The separation of the English colonies of North America
from the mother country, and later on, to a lesser degree, that
of Spanish America from Spain, opened new fields for exploitation by capitalism. The response was not immediate,
doubtless; but enormous possibilities of development existed
in these new countries. This becomes apparent later as the
United States expands and develops industrially. The evolution proves slower there, and takes place at a later date; but
capitalism is destined to triumph in the United States even
more completely than in the older countries of Europe. Having first contributed to the increased wealth of the old countries of Europe, the nations of the Americas are later to become their competitors in the markets of the world.

The underlying causes of the great transformation that
took place in the late eighteenth and early nineteenth centuries can be briefly indicated. For two centuries it had been
considered (and not entirely without reason) that a nation's
wealth depended mainly on the possession of a large monetary
stock. This had been the explanation of Holland's ability to
hold a leading rôle for so long. Holland had relatively few
industries and her territory was small—conditions which less-
ened the quantity and the variety of her natural products,
so that she was forced to carry on only a commission trade. Finally, therefore, she lost the lead to countries like France and
especially England, which, since they were producing manufactured articles for export in increasing quantities, were able
to supply and thus to control numerous markets.

Henceforth, manufacturing industry comes to the forefront. The change is first apparent in England toward the middle of the eighteenth century; and there the change first took place which is more or less accurately called the Industrial Revolution. In France the similar change took place later, though some characteristic signs of the new form of organization appeared toward the end of the *Ancien Régime*. And Colbert's energetic attempt to develop a system of state-aided "manufactures" showed that he possessed, however dimly, a vision of what the future held in store; for, while—as a thousand facts show—industry had been closely subordinated to commercial activity during the two preceding centuries, it was now destined to regulate and, in large measure, to dominate all commercial relations. Industrial capitalism, growing out of commercial capitalism, was destined to become the great phenomenon of modern economic society. The downfall of the colonial system and of the attempt to insure an exclusive monopoly to the mother countries was thus closely related to the advent of the factory system.

In final analysis, it was the maritime and colonial expansion of the European powers which was to prove the most important factor in the genesis of modern capitalism. Did not this expansion give birth to that characteristic phenomenon of the capitalistic society of the nineteenth century, the joint stock company? Did not gambling and speculating in securities follow? With the formation of the Dutch East India Company at the beginning of the seventeenth century, shares in that company became the object of speculative operations, and, in fact, of stock exchange manipulation. Speculators even falsified the news and disseminated rumors in order to affect the price of shares. In England also—but at a later date, since her maritime expansion did not take place so early—creation of stock companies to carry on colonial commerce gave opportunity for speculation in their shares. This frenzy of speculation became particularly bad around 1720, just at the

time when the operations of John Law, also based on oppor-
tunities in colonial commerce, were producing a similar sort
of frenzy in France. This was a time also when the use of
mortgage bonds was begun in Holland. Finally, is it not very
significant that a banking system was first perfected in Holland? The Bank of Amsterdam, the first great state bank,
antedated the Bank of England by almost a century.

It is noteworthy also that the principal stimulus for the
development of industrial capitalism seems to have come
from maritime and colonial commerce. The factory system
appears to have been first developed in the manufacture of
textiles—silks and especially cottons and linens. In truly
prophetic fashion did the anonymous English author of the
Considerations on East Indian Trade show, as early as 1701,
how the importation of merchandise from India might trans-
form industry quite profoundly:

> And thus the East India Trade by producing things with less,
> and consequently cheaper labour, is a very likely way of forcing
> Men upon the invention of Arts and Engines, by which other
> things may be also done with less and cheaper labour and there-
> fore may abate the price of Manufactures, tho' the Wages of Men
> shou'd not be abated.[6]

CHAPTER VIII

THE BEGINNINGS OF INDUSTRIAL CAPITALISM: THE FACTORY SYSTEM

I. COMMERCIAL EXPANSION AND THE INDUSTRIAL REVOLUTION

THE leading rôle played by commercial capitalism has been disclosed in earlier chapters. Its next great contribution to economic life was the stimulation of that great industrial transformation, which came during the second half of the eighteenth century, the transformation we now know by the name of the Industrial Revolution. This occurred first in England, and from there spread to the Continent. But, whereas the English Industrial Revolution always seems to have developed quite spontaneously, the industrial transformation of France is tinged with an element of artificiality; for there, during the *Ancien Régime*, the introduction of machinery and the establishment of the factory system were mainly the result of efforts by the government.[1]

That most illuminating study of Paul Mantoux on the English Industrial Revolution in the eighteenth century shows that the industrial growth of Lancashire was due especially to the progress of Liverpool, a port which at first had been engaged almost exclusively in the colonial trade. The region around Manchester became the center of cotton manufacture because the business men of Liverpool were active in importing raw cotton. The same author also insists—and again quite rightly—on the influence of the improved internal transporta-

VIEW OF LIVERPOOL.

tion upon industrial progress. A network of canals and roads was rapidly extended over England. But this does not seem to have been an influence of more than secondary importance, for France had built roads on a considerable scale during the seventeenth and especially during the eighteenth century. To be sure, this improved transportation system contributed to the transformation of French economic life; but, in the absence of an external stimulus, it was insufficient to overturn the traditional organization. Moreover, while England had been quick to follow the example of Holland, which had amassed wealth in the commission trade, France moved more slowly. By the middle of the century, therefore, England held a favored position in the overseas trade; and it was this trade, rather than internal conditions, which furnished the stimulus to seek means of increasing output and cheapening costs of production. All things considered, therefore, it was natural that the evolution of industry should occur later in France than in England and much less dramatically; and that the industrial transformation of France should lag behind the Industrial Revolution of England.

Commerce was so clearly recognized as the stimulus of industrial activity that the word "commerce" in the seventeenth and eighteenth centuries came to mean manufacturing quite as much as it meant commerce in the strict sense of that word. The same observation holds true of the English word "trade." At that time also, it should be noted, the industrial producer did not solicit orders or seek to accommodate himself to the whims of his customers. Such was the function of the wholesale trader, or exporter. Thus, Magon de la Balue, the shipowner of St.-Malo, placed his orders for silks with the commission houses of Lyons; but he never left off complaining about defective goods, or about the tricks of the manufacturers and their failure to satisfy customers. In Lyons, meanwhile, the master merchants had come into control of the producing organization.

The accumulation of capital was also, in a certain measure, furthered by the progress of manufacturing industry. The woolen industry of England, and especially the export trade in cloth, had given a start to the expansion of trade whereby that country became a considerable maritime power; and, moreover, numerous masters in many branches of trade had become wealthy—so wealthy, indeed, that they held a position quite distinct from that of their fellows. In this fashion, a class of capitalists was recruited from the ranks of those actively engaged in business. This development was by no means confined to England alone; on the contrary, it appeared in other countries as well.

II. THE RURAL AND DOMESTIC INDUSTRY

The influence of commercial capitalism upon manufacturing industry is first seen in the growth of a system of rural and domestic industry,—a phase in the evolution of industry which characterizes the economic history of all the countries of Western Europe. The peasants and agricultural workers used a part of their time in the manufacture of linen or woolen cloth, the business of marketing the finished product, and frequently also of supplying raw materials being undertaken by a member of the merchant class—the merchant-manufacturer. This form of organization appeared in many branches of industry which had previously been confined to the towns; and, beginning with the sixteenth century, it spread over the countryside of the Low Countries.

Thus the signs of commercial capitalism are plainly seen in the progress of the rural manufacturing industry of sixteenth century Belgium; for the merchant-manufacturers, the capitalist-business men of the towns, built up stocks of the manu-

factures turned out by the country artisans and arranged for
their sale abroad. In the country districts of Flanders (the
Walloon country) and of Hainaut, in the neighborhood of
Lille, of Bailleul, and especially of Armentières and of Hond-
schoote, the Spanish wools were being woven into light and
cheap fabrics called "worsted." The English draper soon found
himself unable to compete with these fabrics. The linen industry also spread over the countryside, and the tapestry industry, likewise. Perhaps the most typical example is that
afforded by the manufacture of cheap tapestries, which fed
into the important export market of Antwerp. The making of
the expensive art tapestries, of course, remained in the towns.
At this time (as Professor Pirenne notes) the coal industry
had not yet become capitalistic in form.

The merchant-manufacturer appeared in the English woolen
industry as early as the fifteenth century. His function was to
direct the operations of the country artisans whom he furnished with raw materials (and sometimes even with tools)
and whose product he sold in foreign markets.[2] Indeed, as
Sir William Ashley has said so rightly in his *Economic Organization of England*, the country craftsmen lacked, not the
tools of production, but contact with the markets. Therefore
they were forced to depend upon the merchants for an outlet,
except in Yorkshire where the situation was somewhat different. There, a Committee of the House of Commons showed
in 1806, the rural worker himself bought the wool which he
spun into yarn. This, in turn, he wove into cloth, which he
"finished" and then sold in the markets of the neighboring
towns, notably Bradford, Leeds, Halifax, and Wakefield.
He was an independent master. But in the course of the eighteenth century, even in that section, a growing volume of orders was coming from outside the market towns; and the time
was not far distant when the power of the merchant would
be felt in the actual manufacturing organization.

In the Irish linen industry, which was becoming localized in Ulster, a similar evolution took place. There the weavers were agricultural tenants, and the manufacturing of linen took only a part of their time. In this particular, the Irish linen industry resembled that of Brittany. The finished goods were sold in local markets, such as Belfast or Dublin, or to middlemen who in turn sold to merchants of the cities. In the latter half of the eighteenth century, the workmen gradually fell under the economic control of the merchants, who often sold their cloth directly in England. The position occupied by the merchant-manufacturer became more and more important; and, at the end of the century, the bleachers, who at first had operated on only a small scale, frequently became important masters, exercising control over all the steps in the manufacture. Their efforts resulted in the introduction of machinery for making linens and thus assured the triumph of industrial capitalism in the industry.[3]

In France, two types of rural industry can be readily distinguished. In the first place, there is the rural industry of those regions such as Brittany and Bas-Maine, where the agricultural resources were poor and where there was little urban life. In those provinces, the linen industry of the countryside did not come into severe competition with an urban industry, since but few looms were set up in the towns. The peasants found raw materials close at hand, while the merchants concerned themselves almost exclusively with marketing the finished cloth. They neither undertook the direction of production nor the furnishing of the raw materials; and at most, they merely looked out for the bleaching and finishing of the linen cloth. Only in the exceptional case did they become manufacturers on their own account.

Thus, neither in Brittany nor in Maine did the rural industry give birth to a capitalistic system of enterprise. The loss of the export trade with Cadiz, during the Revolutionary

Wars, brought ruin in its train, and the rural industry fell into a decline at the end of the eighteenth century and early in the nineteenth. Presently the manufacturing of linen disappeared from the countryside.

In other provinces, such as Flanders, Picardy, and Upper Normandy, the situation was very different. In Brittany, agriculture was prosperous, and the urban industry had spread over the neighboring countryside. Here the rural industry developed mainly because many peasants did not own land. Under these circumstances, the rural artisan often depended on merchant-manufacturers who gave him orders for his goods and directions for his work. In any case, the merchants distributed raw materials to the rural workers and often, indeed, furnished them with tools. Their success in developing rural manufacturing even went so far as to threaten the urban workshops with ruin—a condition which led to complaints such as those of the manufacturers and workers of Troyes. Furthermore, at the end of the *Ancien Régime*, these merchant-manufacturers introduced machinery into the knitting and cotton spinning trades, innovations which reacted upon the old urban industry with disastrous effects and increased the competition from the rural industry. The new organization progressed so far in many directions that only one step remained: let the machines be concentrated in a factory and the factory system (*la grande industrie*) would be born. On his part, the merchant-manufacturer would be transformed into a master of industry.

III. THE RÔLE OF COMMERCIAL CONCENTRATION

Commercial capitalism also took hold in the textile industry of the towns, with the result that even artisans who previously had been quite independent were reduced to the position of wage earners. The silk industry around Lyons affords a most striking example of this change.[4] Even in the seventeenth century, there was a distinction between master merchants and master workers, as is shown by the statute of 1667. Less than eighty years later, another statute—that of 1744—defined the position of the master workers as wage earners and subordinates of the merchant class. The latter supplied even designs or patterns, as well as raw materials, and often loaned the funds necessary for the purchase of a stock of tools. Furthermore, the prices paid for the work were fixed by the merchant, though not until after the task had been completed. Thus the position occupied by the worker came to be more and more that of a dependent.

The reasons for this transformation are not hard to find: the merchants who risked their capital were forced to lay down the law to the workers, as output increased and markets expanded. The workers were quite without knowledge of what the market was demanding. In a luxury industry, especially, the merchants performed a function of great importance, since they alone were in position to watch those changes of fashion which are always of great importance in a manufacturing business. Finally, it should be noted that the change in the form of the organization was complete before machinery had been introduced.

The cloth (woolen) industry shows a similar evolution, though one less general in scope. Here the part played by commercial capitalism is readily explained on technical grounds, for the manufacture of cloth requires a variety of quite distinct operations. First the wool must be washed and scoured and next carded and combed. Then comes the spinning, a work chiefly done by women, followed by the winding, spooling and warping. Next comes the weaving; and, before the cloth is ready for market, it must be dyed, napped and sheared, or, if made of carded wool, fulled. The peculiar func-

tion of the merchant in all this work was that of directing the
several processes of manufacture, a task which became still
more necessary as the industry spread over the countryside.
Indeed, the varied rôle of the merchant-manufacturer of cloth
can only be described by a catalogue of his several functions.
These are clearly stated in the following quotation:

> The merchant buys raw wool, has it washed, scoured, and dyed
> by his workers. Sometimes he then gives it directly to the carders
> or spinners; but more often to a small *entrepreneur* (himself a
> worker) who takes it for distribution in his village. When the
> merchant gets the yarn back, he generally prepares the warp
> which, with the woof yarn, he turns over to a second *entrepre-
> neur*, generally a weaver himself, who takes care of the weaving.
> Once the goods are woven, the merchant has the necessary finish-
> ing processes performed by master nappers and shearers. Often-
> times the merchant himself is the owner of a fulling mill.

Concentration of the commercial functions in the hands of
a specialist, the merchant-manufacturer, while complete in the
largest centers, such as Sedan, Rheims, Rouen, and Elbeuf,
at the end of the eighteenth century, was not everywhere manifest. Sometimes, as in Amiens, the work was distributed to a
succession of *entrepreneurs* quite independent of each other;
while in the South, small manufacturers persisted in considerable number.

In the localities where commercial operations had been concentrated in the hands of the merchant-manufacturers, as in
Rheims, there sometimes developed a system of organization
which may be called "industrial concentration," a system of
organization which brought all the steps in the manufacturing
process under the same roof. It was to the interest of the merchant to group the workers under the same roof since this enabled him to supervise the work and at the same time to cut

down transportation costs. Such was the situation of a number of manufacturers in the south of France located at Trivalle, near Carcassonne, for example, or at Villeneuvette, near Clermont-l'Hérault. This development in the cloth industry shows clearly that the system of "industrial concentration" which foreshadowed the coming of the factory was not the result of the introduction of machinery, since the latter change occurred only under the First Empire.[5] At Montauban, a manufacturer erected a building which cost him 125,000 *livres;* at Rheims, more than half the looms were in large factories, while the concentration at Louviers was greater still: fifteen *entrepreneurs* had brought thousands of workers together. The enormous factory built by one of the latter at a cost of 200,-000 *livres* housed five workshops. But even under these circumstances, the independent workman did not disappear entirely.

In the knitted-goods industry, the hold of commercial capitalism on manufacturing operations was the result of the introduction and widespread use of the knitting frames, the cost of which was rather high, some 300–400 *livres.* These were introduced early. Everywhere the master workers were under the control of a few rich merchant-manufacturers. At the end of the *Ancien Régime,* 48 merchants of Lyons gave out work to 819 master workmen; and 55 merchants of Orléans employed 260 such masters.

It is significant that the merchant-manufacturers, even when manufacturing was spread out under the domestic or "putting out" system, could rightly call themselves manufacturers; for the word "manufacture" was often used synonymously with "industry," a word which was then seldom used in the sense which it took on during the nineteenth century.[6] For example, the expression "linen manufactures of Rennes" was used; but, when the work of artisans or craftsmen was referred to, the words "arts and crafts" (*arts et métiers*) were used.

IV. MANUFACTURING INDUSTRY

Thus it seems that manufacturing industry and the factory system have played rôles less important than those often attributed to them—rôles which were emphasized by Karl Marx in *Das Kapital.*

No doubt, the royal manufacturing establishments of France (*les manufactures royales*) and those other enterprises to which special privileges had been granted through the efforts of Colbert, were not without influence on the beginnings of the factory system (*la grande industrie*), even though this development came sometime later. Aided by premiums and official subsidies, these enterprises commanded considerably more capital than most of the others of the times. Therefore, they were able to provide a relatively perfect stock of tools, at least for the finishing operations. Their development was further favored by the monopoly privilege granted to them. This work of Colbert was not wholly without an important effect on the future, therefore, since numerous industrial "islands" emerged. New industries started up in France, and a few of these attained real success. For the most part, however, the manufacturing operations were not concentrated in great establishments. Instead, they were organized on the "putting out" system, utilizing the workers of the countryside on a considerable scale. In this particular, therefore, no significant change can be distinguished during the eighteenth century. Yet it must be recognized that the French manufacturing industry of the time did constitute an important step in the industrial evolution of France. The birth of the factory system and of the machine process—as Charles Ballot has justly remarked—was in great part due to the efforts of the state.

In England, on the contrary, the factory system (*la grande industrie*) sprang up spontaneously; moreover, the existing manufacturing enterprise played a much less important rôle there than in France. The desire for revenues had led the Stuarts to create certain monopolies, such, for example, as those created to engage in the manufacture of soap, of steel wire, and of playing cards. But the nation protested vigorously against these monopolies, and the mercantilist policy supported, in fact even created, by the Stuart monarchy, disappeared with it. The policy of *laissez-faire* triumphed. The influence of the Revolution of 1688 was also of the first importance, for it favored the cause of commercial and economic liberty. This explains why the efforts to establish textile mills were not numerous in the eighteenth century and did not meet with great success.

V. TECHNICAL PROGRESS AND INDUSTRIAL CONCENTRATION

Industrial concentration (the development of large scale manufacturing units, without which there could have been no modern industry) was born of technical necessity. A typical example is afforded by the printing of calico. In the printing of calico, large scale operations had been undertaken even before the introduction of machinery, strictly speaking. This development is readily understood if we accept the explanation of Charles Ballot that "the technical conditions of manufacture called for the investment of considerable capital, the assembly of workers in shops, and the establishment of a system of division of labor." Large buildings were required for the workshops, large rooms for drying the cloth, and extensive fields for bleaching it. The equipment of tools was complicated and costly; large stocks of cloth and of dyes were needed. Moreover, the variety of operations in the same shop called for a division of tasks among the numerous groups of specialized hands working under the same roof. Therefore, it is not surprising that, towards the end of the *Ancien Ré-*

gime, there were more than 100 establishments in this industry, producing printed cloth to a value in excess of 12,000,000 *livres*. For the most part, these establishments were the property of companies with several partners; but many belonged to very wealthy stock companies. In 1789, the well-known Oberkampf Company, for example, had a capital of almost 9,-000,000 *livres* and its 1792 profits were 1,581,000 *livres*. The printing of calico by machine did not begin until 1797, however.

VI. THE INTRODUCTION OF MACHINERY

Yet the concentration of industry and population, which are necessary conditions of a great capitalistic industry, must have awaited the triumph of machinery. Machinery was first introduced into silk throwing: machines had been rather well perfected as early as the first half of the eighteenth century by the Jubiés. Then, in the second half of that century came the inventions of Vaucanson, which the Deydiers of Aubenas sought to put to practical use. The success of these technical improvements explains why numerous large establishments, such as those of the Jubiés at Sône, developed in the throwing branch of the silk industry, whereas silk spinning remained a domestic and rural industry until well into the nineteenth century.

It remained for a new industry—the manufacture of cotton cloth—to witness the development and rapid introduction of machinery during the eighteenth century. The mechanical inventions first appeared in England, where that industry had secured a start much earlier than elsewhere. The first invention was the flying shuttle of Kay (1733). This speeded up weaving and created the need for a large quantity of yarn. How increase the production of yarn? To meet the need thus created, machines for spinning cotton were invented; the jenny in 1765, the water-frame of Arkwright two years later, and then the mule of Crompton. France was very backward in the invention of cotton machinery; it proved necessary to bring both workmen and machines from England.

The jenny was run by hand and thus could be used by isolated spinners. Therefore it was not a menace to the rural industry. The mule, on the contrary, and other "continuous machines" tended to bring about industrial concentration. In France, as in England, this fact stands out clearly. Even before the Revolution, there was a certain number of factories in France: those of Lecler at Brives, of Martin and Flesselles at Amiens, the enterprises started by the Duke of Orleans and Montargis, and the establishment of Louviers. In the first years of the Revolution, the movement toward bringing industrial operations under the factory system was accelerated; but in general it was not until the time of the Empire that the spinning of cotton became a factory industry. The talent for organization possessed by such men as Bauwens and Richard-Lenoir, and their wealth, contributed greatly to this change.

The introduction of machinery into the woolen industry of France, as into that of England, proved more tardy, despite Cartwright's invention of the power loom. The transformation in France took place mainly during the Napoleonic period; and the credit for this change is due to great industrial figures such as Ternaux "who covered France with factories and Europe with counting houses."

As a matter of fact, so far as the textile industry alone is concerned, it is apparent that, even in England, the evolution of industry was far from complete at the beginning of the nineteenth century. Power spinning was slow to get established, even in the cotton industry, and the introduction of machinery into the linen industry came very late. Not until the Monarchy of July (1830–48) did the introduction of machinery bring about the transformation of the French linen industry. In the secondary industries, such as the manufacture of glass and paper, some important technical improvements were achieved before the Revolution. But there were only a few large factories, such as the paper mill of Montgolfier at Annonay; and the great majority of the enterprises were small affairs which employed only a few men.

In the beginning, "machinery played only a secondary part in the most decisive transformation" which occurred in the metallurgical industries—the substitution of coal for wood in smelting. This change in technique stimulated the founding of such large establishments as the Creusot works which was a capitalistic enterprise from the start. But, in general, the transition took place only slowly. Such was especially the case in France, where it continued well into the second half of the last century. At the time of the Revolution, the great majority of the metallurgical works were small scale plants employing only a few men. For a long time, the industry was quite widely scattered; and since, for the most part, wood was still used as fuel in making pig iron, the industry remained in the wooded regions.

In England, on the contrary—where, because of the lack of wood, the coke process of smelting iron had been introduced early—large metallurgical establishments developed as early as the first half of the eighteenth century. But small workshops continued to persist in the hardware industries (locksmith and cutlery works) for a long time, especially at Birmingham. Even in France the machine process had fostered the rapid growth of the iron working industries, such as rolling mills, machine tool plants, and machine shops (*ateliers de construction*). These were especially stimulated by the growing demands of the factory system in the textile industry.

The introduction of mechanical means for developing power took place only very slowly. At first, water power was used in France, as it had been in England. But everywhere in the latter country, the steam engine tended to displace water power. Such, indeed, was the situation as early as the end of the eighteenth century. In France, on the other hand, there were very few steam engines as late as 1789, the only exceptions being the "fire engines" installed for pumping out the mines and for operating hoisting machinery. More than half a century must elapse before the steam engine is found in general use by French industry.

The steam engine represents one of the first applications of science to industry. In general, such applications seem to have lagged behind such technical inventions as have been the fruits of intuition or genius, or the result of a long process of experimentation. Yet as early as the beginning of the nineteenth century, it was becoming apparent that chemistry would prove the science which would suggest the greatest number of industrial improvements.

What precedes suggests that, while only the widespread introduction of machinery could assure the triumph of the factory system (*la grande industrie*), the development of large industrial plants appears to have been due rather to the multiplicity of essential technical operations in the various manufacturing industries themselves. In the textile industry, for example, the tendency toward bringing operations under a single roof arose from the complexity of the industrial process. This condition made the intervention of commercial capitalism quite indispensable; again in calico printing, conditions peculiar to that manufacture necessitated the factory. Here the introduction of machinery did nothing except to intensify a transformation already accomplished, or well on the way of being accomplished.

VII. THE CHARACTER OF INDUSTRIAL CAPITALISM

Whoever takes the time to examine the economic history of the eighteenth century will see clearly that it was not in the industries where the machine had been farthest developed that the enterprises tended to take on a capitalistic form. On the contrary, it was in those which, by their very nature, called for heavy expenditures for equipment and operations. The mining industry (and especially the coal industry) affords a striking example of this. At first the French mines had been exploited by their owners or by small business men; but this resulted in such inefficiency that the government, by the Decree of 1744, decided that no mine should be exploited without a royal concession. The owners and the small *entrepreneurs* were often dispossessed for the benefit of outsiders and especially for the benefit of large companies, like the company of Anzin described in the following paragraph. Only companies possessing considerable resources were able to introduce the necessary technical improvements such as the making of borings, the opening of galleries and air shafts for ventilation, the pumping of water from the pits—improvements which required large capital if they were to be carried out scientifically. The use of steam engines (*pompes à feu*) was also spreading in the mining industry.

These companies—joint stock companies, and limited partnerships, chiefly companies *en commandite* or *en nom collectif*—had the essential characteristics of large capitalistic enterprises. Such, for example, were the companies of Alais, Carmaux and Anzin. As early as 1756, the Anzin Company, operating in the North of France, employed 1,000 miners and 500 other workers in its shops. By 1789 it was employing 4,000 men and had opened 1,800 to 2,400 feet of galleries. Twelve steam engines were used. In that year, 3,750,000 quintals

of coal were mined, and the commercial profits were 1,200,-
000 *livres*, a figure 100 per cent in excess of the expenses. In
other branches of mining, the capitalistic character of the enterprises is less impressive; but stock companies were often
formed by wealthy financiers or merchants (*négociants*) or
shipowners, to carry on such ventures; and in their lists of
stockholders were to be found the names of noblemen and
magistrates, just as was the case in coal mining.

In the cotton industry, on the contrary, the stock company
was seldom found, even after machinery had triumphed. Limited partnerships (*sociétés en commandite*) there often were;
but most of the factories belonged to individual proprietors
who had recourse to borrowings and who sought the good offices of the bankers. It is not possible to say with certainty
where their capital came from.

The beginning of the eighteenth century saw a large number
of stock companies, or at least limited partnerships (*compagnies en commandite*) in the calico-printing industry. This condition grew out of the tendency toward integration which began to manifest itself in an industry already strongly marked
by a capitalistic character. The following is a very apt description of this state of affairs: "Very often manufacturers
combine the weaving and spinning of cloth with its printing.
This they do very willingly because such extension of their
operations does not call for an increase of capital, and they
'put out' that part of the work over the countryside. While
they are heads of factories (or almost such) for the printing
operations, they perform the function of the merchant-
manufacturer for the making of cloth." Under the Empire,
most of the great mills for spinning cotton belonged to great
industrialists who carried on weaving and even printing.

On the other hand, the development of industry and the introduction of machinery did lead to the growth of specialization; and the different operations of manufacturing gave rise

to specialized establishments. Especially was this the case with spinning mills: manufacturers, like Boyer-Fonfrède, who had both weaving and spinning mills, now concentrated their efforts on spinning, while, before the advent of machinery, the operations of spinning had been subordinated to those of weaving.

Another consequence, clearly apparent during the Napoleonic period, was the multiplication of their establishments by certain especially enterprising industrialists, such as Bauwens in Belgium, or Richard-Lenoir who set up spinning and weaving plants in Picardy and all over Normandy. An even more striking example is that of Ternaux, who established textile plants all over France, and who built new mills outside Sedan, Rheims, and Louviers, the seats of his principal manufacturing operations.

Commercial activities came to be subordinated to those of manufacturing at this point, as a result of the development of large scale operations in industry. The important industrialist reached out to find new outlets for his products and to become an important trader on his own account. As early as the eighteenth century, manufacturers of calico were carrying on commercial transactions, in the regular course of business. Their activities have been characterized as follows: "They sent agents to buy direct either white cloth at Lorient, the port of the East India Company, or dyed materials in other ports. The most important of them sold to merchants, or even direct to the public. Several manufacturers had stores in Paris, while still others who exported to Germany, to the northern countries, to the colonies, had far flung interests."

It has often been said that the development of a system of industrial concentration (*la concentration industrielle*) brought about the division of labor. But division of labor is an expression which must be defined carefully: for there was a system of division of labor before the tendency toward bringing industrial operations under a single roof was important, if the phrase refers to that multiplicity of technical operations and of trades which is more justly called the division of manufacturing between a large number of crafts. In such case, the division of labor often stimulated the desire to bring operations under a single roof, since this in turn would result in diminished costs of production. But very often, a system of division of labor between steps in the manufacturing process existed for a long time without bringing about concentration in a single plant. Thus, small specialized shops continued to be characteristic of the cutlery industry of Thiers well into the second half of the nineteenth century. But the tendency toward concentration—or, to express it better, the gathering under the same roof of a large number of workers—necessarily produces what Bücher calls the "subdivision of labor" (*Arbeitszerlegung*); in a factory (*atelier concentré*), each worker has his particular job and carries on a small part of the whole manufacturing process. This results in saving time and reducing costs of production.

Another result of the coming of large scale industry (*la grande industrie*)—no less important—was the notable increase in population and the shift in its density. This phenomenon had full play in England, where not only did the population increase in large proportions, but where an entirely new England—that of the north and the west—surged ahead of the old England of the southern counties. Nothing comparable with this occurred in France. But there also the industrial transformation did lead to an increase of urban population, at the expense of the rural districts. The shift was of much smaller proportions than in England; and, when the country as a whole is considered, the old equilibrium is seen to have been maintained. Such proved the case because France has remained, to a great extent, an agricultural country. The Industrial Revolution wrought no violent or sudden change in France. Moreover it came much later there than in England, where, at least in the cotton industry, it triumphed during the last twenty years of the eighteenth century. Often the same people—Samuel Oldknow for example—who were still merchant-manufacturers around 1780, were presently busy starting large spinning mills to employ several hundred workers.

Yet the great industrial transformation which took place was less a *revolution*, in the phrase started by Toynbee, than a rapid and irresistible evolution, according to the happy formula of Sir William Ashley.[7] Such should, I believe, be the impression gathered by the reader from the discussion of the preceding pages. On the vast stage of economic history, no sudden shift of scene takes place.[8] Even as early as the sixteenth century some industries—such as the exploitation of mineral resources—had taken on the form of capitalistic enterprise; and, on the other hand, the old scheme of organization dominated by the craftsmen did not suddenly disappear from the scene. Indeed, the craftsmen continued to survive even in the era which marks the triumph of industrial capitalism.

CHAPTER IX

THE PROGRESS OF CAPITALISM IN THE NINETEENTH CENTURY

I**T would be a grave error to think that capitalism held a predominant place in the economic organization at the beginning of the nineteenth century, even in those countries where the economic evolution had progressed fastest.

I. ECONOMIC CONSEQUENCES OF THE FRENCH REVOLUTION

The gigantic wars of the Napoleonic era, following the turmoil of the Revolution, brought the greater part of Europe into the field. In a certain measure, this condition served to precipitate the evolution of capitalism; but, in other respects, notably by hindering maritime and colonial commerce, it retarded that evolution. So far as France is concerned, the economic results of the Revolution (and of the war provoked by it) seem somewhat contradictory. On the one hand, the closing of the ports hit the textile industries which produced for the export market, notably the silk and linen industries. France was no longer able to send linen to Cadiz or the Antilles. On the other hand, the Continental blockade, by closing the French market to English products, stimulated the expansion of the French woolen and cotton industries. The beet sugar industry was created, and the metallurgical industries enjoyed fair prosperity. The French cotton industry was handicapped, however, since France experienced great difficulty in securing supplies of raw cotton, whereas England—the mistress of the seas—had easy access to such supplies. French maritime commerce suffered far more than the English; and, in the end, her traders and merchants grew weary of a government which paid so little attention to their interests. The economic activity of England was but momentarily slowed down by the wars of the years, 1793 to 1815; France, on the other hand, was greatly handicapped in the race with her age-long rival.

II. RAPID PROGRESS OF CAPITALISM IN ENGLAND

Though all the characteristics of the capitalistic régime were apparent in England by 1815, the old organization of industry still had the upper hand—from a quantitative point of view, at least. As Hobson remarks, the changes in the localization of industry were not yet complete, the export trade was still relatively unimportant, and capital and labor were not yet measured by very great numerical quantities.

Conditions in Great Britain were especially favorable to the development of large scale operations in the iron and steel industry. Close to the sea and in close proximity to each other were ample supplies of coal and iron ore. By 1815, coal mining was being carried forward on a considerable scale, although exploitation of the mines through large scale operations, such as require a considerable capital investment, had not yet gone as far in mining as might have been expected. The number of workmen had grown considerably and the number of "steam pumps" had been multiplied; but the conditions of labor had not changed greatly. The smelting branch of the iron industry grew in importance, both in the number of blast furnaces and in output; but large scale operations did not triumph everywhere; and small workshops continued to persist in the making of such objects as cutlery and toys.

Is the factory system and the triumph of industrial capitalism more marked in the textile industry? The cotton manufacture can be considered separately. In 1815, most of the cotton spinning was being done in large scale establishments (*établissements concentrés*) in which the machine had triumphed. The weaving of cotton, on the other hand, was done mainly in small workrooms and in the home. The hand loom weavers—since they consented to accept low wages—held on everywhere, despite the invention of Cartwright's machine, which dates from 1795. Finally the industry was still dominated by the merchant-manufacturers (*marchands-entrepreneurs*), as in the preceding century. In the manufacture of Irish linen, the evolutionary tendency looking toward the triumph of the factory was still but dimly foreshadowed; and, while machines were beginning to appear in the woolen industry of the southwest of England, the domestic industry predominated everywhere else, even in the spinning of yarn. Only 8,000 out of a total of 466,000 pieces of cloth manufactured in Yorkshire came from factories in 1806. The transition was still less advanced in the knitting industry.

In another important particular—the credit organization—the position of England was superior to that anywhere else. There were over 750 country banks in England, though these banks were operated for the most part by small companies. Large financial resources were possessed by only a single institution—the Bank of England. Consequently industry failed to find all the credit needed to expand operations rapidly; and, in times of crisis, it experienced serious financial embarrassment, especially in 1815 when the exchanges were unfavorable as a consequence of the inflation of the currency.

The new organization of industry made steady progress, however; and a sign of this progress was the legislative triumph of industrial liberty, which established the freedom of contract. This was first marked, in 1813, when the statute giving Justices of the Peace the right to fix wages was abro-

gated, and then, in 1814, by the abrogation of the apprenticeship regulations.

But it is during the interval 1815–1850 that the capitalistic organization of industry really triumphs in England. The
factory system and the use of machinery then make rapid
progress in the cotton manufacture, and there production increases in the largest proportions. Cotton goods come to make
up half of England's exports. Even the linen industry fell
under the sway of the factory system and the machinery process. The metallurgical industries underwent a comparable
transformation; whereas the old forms of organization persisted in the woolen industry, despite the notable success in the
invention of new machinery. Some progress was achieved, to
be sure; but, as Professor Clapham has shown in his recent remarkable work, no sudden revolution occurred.[1] Indeed, the
transition was slower than is ordinarily believed. The old
organization was able to hold on until 1850; and, even at that
comparatively late date, the hand weavers were still very
numerous and large establishments were in the minority. The
triumph of industrial capitalism was not finally achieved until
the second half of the nineteenth century.

On the other hand, it is true that—especially after 1836—
the somewhat feverish construction of a great number of railroad lines tended to revolutionize the whole system of internal
communication and to hasten the industrial transformation.
Further sign of all this change appears in the progress of the
coal industry: coal exports rose from 250,000 tons in 1828 to
2,100,000 tons in 1845. Still another sign was the enormous
increase in raw-material imports: cotton imports rose from 51
million pounds in 1813 to 490 millions in 1841, and imports
of raw wool rose from 9,775,000 pounds in 1820 to 49 million
pounds in 1840.

The tendency to build up business enterprises commanding
a considerable capital—what may be called the tendency to-

ward capitalistic concentration (*concentration capitaliste*)—
was reflected in the creation of innumerable joint stock companies. Over six hundred such—insurance companies, water-
works, gas plants, mines, canals, ports, improvements, and
railroads—were founded between 1822 and 1850. These represented a capital of a half billion pounds sterling. Private
banks lost ground, and banking companies (of which England
already possessed thirty in 1833 and Ireland, three) pushed
ahead. Moreover, seventy-two banking companies were
founded in England between 1833 and 1836, and ten in Ireland. All of these issued notes. As a consequence of this flowering of capitalism, a great speculation was stimulated and
serious crises followed. The depressing effects of the crisis
which broke in 1825 continued to be felt as late as 1832.

Does this mean that by 1850 the triumph of industrial capitalism was complete in England? By no means. Small scale
operations were still numerous. The knitting workers of Leicester, the cotton weavers of Lancashire, and the wool weavers
of Norwich and of Bradford continued to work in their homes
for starvation wages, wages only an eighth of those received
by workers employed in large scale plants (*la grande industrie*). From these groups were recruited the mobs which
wrecked so many machines in 1835; and from them, in 1839,
came the adherents of Chartism.

By 1850, capitalistic industry was playing a very important
rôle, however; and this is the reason why England was the first
country to pass factory acts, the broad outlines of which had
been laid down by 1850. Passage of the Ten Hour Law in
1847 was a decisive event.

III. THE SLOWER PROGRESS OF FRANCE

The evolution of capitalism progressed more slowly in
France during the first half of the nineteenth century than

in England. On the morrow of the Revolution, though legal institutions had been profoundly changed, economic life remained much as it had been under the *Ancien Régime*. The course of the Revolution had often resulted in an impoverishment of the towns and France remained essentially an agricultural country. Trade remained dull, credit was very badly disorganized, and means of communication were often more difficult than before the Revolution. Bankers were few and recourse to usurers was frequently necessary. Finally, manufacturing industry lacked qualified workmen, and technical improvements were few.

In the case of the metallurgical industry, also, the old practices persisted, although some large factories, like that of Fourchambaut, had been established, and the plant of the Schneider family at Le Creusot had a fairly modern equipment. But the process of smelting with coke was still but little known and charcoal was still generally used in smelting ore. As late as 1840, indeed, the coke process was employed in only 41 of the French blast furnaces out of a total of 462; but the transformation became more rapid after 1840 and especially in the years following 1850. Thereafter, the development of large plants made great progress. From 1830 to 1848, the consumption of coal quadrupled.

Meanwhile, the woolen manufacture showed but little resemblance to the modern factory system; at Rheims, for example, small workshops continued to dominate the industry. At Louviers, on the other hand, there were a few fine factories at the time of the Restoration, and the mechanical spinning of combed wool developed greatly under the Monarchy of July (1830–1848). But in France, as in England, large scale operations made the greatest progress in the cotton manufacture, especially with the spread of machinery in the weaving branch of that industry. By 1846, there were 31,000 power looms in France.

Still another significant fact is that in 1847 France possessed some 5,000 steam engines (60,000 horse power). Fifty
years later there were 100,000 such—some two and a half million horse power. By 1848, also, there were about a hundred
mechanical paper mills, instead of four, as in 1827.

Clear signs of the progress of the new industrial organization are reflected in the decadence of the rural and domestic
industry: thus, the manufacture of linen disappeared almost
entirely from Brittany and from the department of Mayenne.
These became exclusively agricultural sections. In other
regions, such as Flanders and Picardy, the transformation took
place much more slowly, though the rural industry was destined ultimately to give way to the factory system. The case
of the Vivarais is rather exceptional; here silk spinning continued to be, in part, a family industry; and the transformation from the rural and domestic system to the factory was
not completed until the later half of the nineteenth century.[2]

At all events, small scale manufacturing continued to play
an important rôle in France around the middle of the nineteenth century. In Paris, for example, it was still the predominant industrial form, and in most of the small towns, also,
craftsmen and small masters still held sway.[3] In certain industries, like the glove manufacture of Grenoble, the factory
system did not really manifest itself until the end of the nineteenth century.

Commercial and financial activity also developed quite
slowly in France during the first half of the nineteenth century.

In the first place, the long series of wars after the Revolution and under the Empire had practically annihilated the
French colonial empire. The French overseas commerce also
suffered, and at best its recovery could be only gradual. The
initiative and energy of certain shipowners, notably those of
Bordeaux, led to attempts to reëstablish the old trade rela-

tions or to create new ones with the regions of the Pacific and the Far East; and, in spite of the protectionist régime, which was unfriendly to foreign commerce, these attempts to develop new trading relations did make progress. Appreciable success had been achieved by 1830, and the progress was greatly accelerated under the Monarchy of July (1830–1848). The tonnage of ships entering French ports had amounted to 690,000 tons in 1820; it rose to a million tons in 1830, and to 2,300,-000 tons in 1845.

In the fields of credit and banking, the rate of progress was still slower, especially under the Restoration. The Bank of France continued to be the principal credit institution, though corporations with fairly considerable capitals at their disposal set up certain important provincial banks. One such had been started in Bordeaux by 1818, others in Rouen and Nantes at about the same time; and then, from 1835 to 1838, came the founding of the banks of Lyons, Marseilles, Lille, Havre, Toulouse, and Orléans. In 1830, the Bank of France discounted notes to the amount of 239 millions of francs; in 1840 the figure was 251 millions, while the provincial banks discounted some 60 millions. In 1848 the Bank of France discounted notes to the amount of 288 millions, and the other banks, notes to the amount of 90 millions of francs. The great credit establishments, the *Crédit mobilier*, the *Comptoir d'escompte*, and the *Crédit lyonnais*, were not established and developed until the latter half of the century.

There was another class of bankers (called the *haute banque*), notably the House of Rothschild, which was concerned principally with government financing. Negotiation of state loans had been fairly difficult even as late as the beginning of the nineteenth century; and Prussia, when indebted to Napoleon, had experienced the greatest difficulty in finding lenders even in Holland. But government borrowings multiplied in the course of the century and contributed greatly to the progress of financial capitalism. Activity on the *Bourse* also increased, mainly as a result of speculation induced by the establishment of railroad companies. Even at this time, however, the day of the triumph of financial capitalism still lay in the future.

Commercial publicity also made great progress under the Monarchy of July. Emile de Girardin, anticipating the profits which would accrue from advertisements, hit upon the idea of establishing a low priced newspaper. In 1836, therefore, he formed a corporation with a capital of 800 millions (with shares of 250 francs each) to publish *La Presse*. In the same year *Le Siècle* was established with a capital of 600 millions (shares, 200 francs). *La Presse* soon had 20,000 subscribers. This "industrialization" of the press constituted a veritable revolution: all the other newspapers followed the lead, and between 1836 and 1845 there were some 1,600 newspapers of one kind or the other founded in Paris alone.

IV. ECONOMIC RENAISSANCE OF BELGIUM

Meanwhile, the economic progress of Belgium had disclosed significant evidence of the growth of capitalism there. The Spanish domination during the sixteenth century had brought great suffering upon that country; and even her agriculture had not recovered from the effects of the depression until the eighteenth century. The renaissance of her industry began under the First Empire, but presently—thanks to her rich resources of coal, her geographic situation, and the industrious quality of her inhabitants—Belgium began to move ahead even more rapidly than did France. The metallurgical industries and cotton manufacturing became especially active. As early as 1822, the King of the Netherlands had created an institution to provide credit for commerce and industry (the *Société générale pour favoriser le commerce et l'industrie*), and this institution proved very useful in serving such ends. Indeed, this Belgium institution can be considered as the forerunner of the French *Crédit mobilier* which was not created until much later; for, as Chlepner says, it "learned the way to extend industrial credit and to participate in the creation of joint stock companies." Thus it inaugurated the system of mixed banking, the so-called *"banque mixte,"* a system wrongly believed to have been invented in Germany.

The Bank of Belgium, founded in 1835, had much the same character, though its embarrassment in 1838 delayed the economic progress of the country for a time. But presently the construction of railroads, beginning in 1844, stimulated a new industrial expansion. This period of activity was in turn ended by a new crisis, that of 1847 to 1848, which proved less severe in Belgium than in France, however. In 1850, following this crisis, the *Banque Nationale Belge*, which received the monopoly of the note issue, was founded. As a consequence, the Société Générale and the other banks turned more and more to the business of extending credit to industry. The economic and financial expansion of Belgium was stimulated thereby; and joint stock companies, the development of which had been hindered before 1850 by the hostility of the Catholic party and the advanced liberals, increased in number. Around 1850, therefore, it could be foreseen that Belgium was sure to be one of the centers of European capitalism.

V. PERSISTENCE OF THE OLD ECONOMY IN CENTRAL, EASTERN, AND WESTERN EUROPE

The countries of central Europe, on the other hand, felt the incidence of capitalism only slightly during the first half of the nineteenth century.

In Germany, the old economy still persisted. A good proof of this statement is that in 1816 the rural population of Prussia represented 73 per cent of the total population; and this percentage was 71 per cent even as late as 1852. Moreover, small scale industry (*la petite industrie*) occupied a much larger place there than in France. In certain German towns, 80 or even 90 per cent of the masters employed neither journeyman nor apprentice. In 1816, if the evidence of the Prussian statistics be accepted, there are only 56 employees (journeymen or apprentices) for each 100 masters, and in 1843 only 76. Not until 1845 did a Prussian ordinance (the *Allgemeine Gewerbeordnung*) deprive the guilds of their compulsory character and practically establish the principle of freedom of labor. Even in the most highly industrialized regions, capitalism manifested itself only under the form of the "putting out" system (*Verlagsystem*) : such was the case in the Rhineland, in Westphalia and in Saxony. The old character of the rural industry, especially in the textile manufacture, had been preserved; so far as the organization of industry was concerned, Prussian economic life might still have been functioning in the eighteenth century.

Large scale enterprise made so little progress in Germany that, even if the Westphalian, Saar, and Silesian coal mines be included, there were only 7,500 steam horse power in all Germany in 1837; and only 22,000 horse power in 1846, of which more than half (14,000 horse power) were to be found in mining and metallurgical operations. Yet even in the latter industry, establishments were, for the most part, small affairs. Furthermore, coal mining was still relatively unimportant. Exploitation of the mines in the Ruhr was just beginning in 1815; and fairly active work in the Silesian coal fields began only around 1840. In 1846, the total output of the Prussian mines—despite the richness of their veins—was only about 3,200,000 English tons, while the French mines were producing 4,500,000 tons.

In 1831 there were only 25,500 looms in the German cotton industry, and of these only 4 per cent were power looms. Nor were spinning machines numerous—whether for spinning wool, hemp, or even cotton. In a word, the textile industry continued to be mainly a source of extra income for the German peasant; in England and France, on the other hand, the cotton industry was very active, and the factory already well established.

In Germany, moreover, the industrial transformations which were certain to insure the ultimate triumph of capitalism were mainly the work of the governments. Particularly was this true of Prussia where the government created the Trade Institute (*Gewerbe Institut*), and, by taking the lead in the Customs Union (*Zollverein*), prepared the way for the economic unity of Germany. Around the middle of the century, however, Germany was still mainly a country of peasants and craftsmen.

The German credit organization was also still rather primitive. The principal banking institution of Prussia was a state institution—the Bank of Prussia. In 1834 the Bank of Bavaria was founded and in 1838 the Bank of Leipzig, both of which prospered and both of which contributed to the economic expansion of Germany in the succeeding period. Private banks played only a slight rôle except in Frankfort, which was still the great financial market of Germany. Capitalism was even less well developed in the various countries of the Austrian monarchy. These had not yet emerged from the feudal régime and the city of Vienna alone was an important financial market.

Finally, the influence of capitalism had been very little felt in the Russian Empire, which, except for a part of Poland, was almost exclusively engaged in agriculture. There was some manufacturing in certain areas, notably at Moscow, but these were "hot house" creations; and large scale industrial operations were still unimportant. The rôle played by the great fair at Nijni-Novgorod is another bit of evidence showing that economic life in Russia for the most part still resembled that of the Middle Ages. Indeed, such few effects of capitalism as were then being felt in Russia came mainly from outside, as a result of the growth of foreign trade. The export trade in wheat contributed in notable degree to increasing the quantity of capital which later served in the development of capitalism.

In southern Europe, in Italy, in Spain, and in Portugal, the old economic régime still persisted; and, except for the building up of important manufacturing industries in Catalonia, the old régime was destined to persist for a long time.

VI. CAPITALISM IN THE UNITED STATES

Capitalism, which has developed so marvelously in the United States in the last fifty years, was but getting its start during the first half of the nineteenth century. In the Northern States large scale industry, the factory system, had begun to implant itself, at least in the textile industry; and the number of factories was increased rapidly in that section, especially after 1825. In the metal industries, on the other hand, and in coal mining, operations were still on a fairly modest scale. The United States continued to depend on Europe, and notably on England, for supplies of manufactured goods, despite the protective tariffs of 1816 and 1834. The reason for this dependence is readily understood, when it is recalled that the Americans were still occupied with clearing the immense territories west of the mountains; their economic expansion was therefore certain to be *extensive* rather than *intensive*.

The Southern States, where cotton growing flourished, were almost exclusively agricultural in their economic life; and their agriculture was carried on mainly with slave labor.

Even in this period, however, the great increase of ways and means of communication pointed to the future development. Numerous roads were created, at least in the East; the Erie Canal was finished in 1825, opening up a through route between the Seaboard and the Great Lakes and then, beginning in 1830, came the construction of railroads. The very fact that the road and turnpike system of the United States was still primitive and but scantily developed resulted in a more rapid and more intense building of railroads there than on the continent of Europe, or even in England. The application of steam to navigation enabled the United States to push ahead of Europe in its use of modern means of transportation; and the completion of the Erie Canal was followed by that of the Pennsylvania and Ohio canal systems in the next decades. The Mississippi and its principal tributaries also became important highways of commerce. Internal commerce became very active. It may be said, therefore, that though capitalism developed more slowly in the United States than in the more advanced countries of the Old World, the growing accumulation of capital ensured the capitalistic future of the great American Republic.

VII. THE TRIUMPH OF CAPITALISM PREPARED BY THE
TRANSFORMATION OF MEANS OF COMMUNICATION

It was the transformation in the means of communication during the first half of the nineteenth century which opened the way for the triumph of capitalism during the second half of the century. Except in England, however, where the effects were felt earlier to a moderate degree, the economic consequences of the revolution occasioned by the development of

steam navigation and the railroad did not make themselves
felt until the latter half of the century. The construction of
the great French railroad lines was not begun until 1842.[4]
The German railroad system was also slow to develop: by
1851, only 3,000 miles of railroad had been opened there,
while the French mileage was some 2,000 miles. Moreover,
the influence of the new means of communication was still
more marked in Germany than in France. The changes
created by improved transportation proved even more tardy
in Russia and in all Eastern Europe.

<h3 style="text-align:center">VIII. SLIGHT INFLUENCE OF CAPITALISM ON
AGRICULTURE</h3>

Everywhere in Europe, agriculture has been the last economic interest to be affected by capitalism. In certain measure,
England affords an exception to this rule; for the disappearance of small holdings, and the creation of great landed
estates have resulted in large scale farming in that country.
The British tenant farmer is a very different sort of person
from the French or German peasant. He generally has a
substantial amount of capital at his disposal and he carries on
agriculture much as he would an industrial enterprise.[5]

On the Continent, the change has worked out very differ-
ently. There the effects of the rise of prices (to which Sombart attaches such great importance) were hardly felt in the
first half of the nineteenth century. In France the price of
wheat remained practically unchanged from 1815 to 1850;
and only in the second half century did ground rents increase
greatly.

Therefore, the rural economic life of France continued to
bear a very considerable resemblance to that of the *Ancien
Régime*—especially until around 1840—though the social
condition of the peasants had been improved by the destruc-

tion of the seigniorial régime and by the sale of national properties, both fruits of the Revolution. But practically the same old agricultural methods persisted, despite the creation of artificial meadows (*prairies artificielles*) through the introduction of such forage crops as clover and lucerne, and despite the fairly numerous new clearings and the spread of some new crops, the potato, for example. Only in the richest sections of France did notable improvement take place; in the backward regions, the rate of progress was still very slow.

Not until 1840 did the transformation of French agriculture really begin to get under way; but even this movement failed to attain its full proportions until after 1860. The improvement of transportation here played a rôle of the first order, though the application of science to agriculture must also be taken into account. Another favorable circumstance grew out of the Revolution of July: it resulted in the retirement into the countryside of the class of noble proprietors who, for the most part, were legitimists.

The course of the evolution does not seem to have been very different in Germany, especially in Western and Southern Germany. There the system of rural and domestic industry was preserved even longer than in France and, as Sombart has shown, it remained prosperous until around 1850. Only on the great aristocratic estates of East Prussia did a more rapid change occur. The landed proprietors were able to apply more capital to agriculture and to treat their operations (the management of which they kept in their own hands) much as they would treat operations in an industrial establishment. In Russia, where the régime of serfdom and the *mir* was still perpetuated, agriculture preserved even more of its primitive character.[6]

Agriculture in the United States presented special considerations: for here was a new country with a great variety of soil and climate. Thus, at one time, several stages in agricultural progress could be found there: a primitive type of agriculture, a system of allowing land to lie fallow, and the scientific rotation of crops. In the first half of the century, however, agricultural operations were mainly extensive as the frontier pushed westward, and therefore farming did not fall under the sway of capitalism.[7]

In a word, agriculture around 1850 was still under the old family economy; it did not begin to be "industrialized" and "commercialized" until the second half of the century. And even in the twentieth century—except in the United States—agriculture has been influenced by capitalism only in limited measure. Agriculture has not yet fallen completely under the domination of industry and commerce. The technique of farming has been transformed in large part, but the very nature of farm work tends to preserve intact many of the traits of the old economic and social organization which have pretty much disappeared in other branches of economic life.

IX. CONCLUSION

Thus, the advent of the capitalistic régime was clearly apparent by the middle of the nineteenth century, though the supremacy of capitalism was not yet an accomplished fact. Its hour of final triumph lay still farther ahead. Even in the countries where the evolution had gone very far, many traces of the old organization still persisted. Large scale operations were by no means universal in industry. Cartels and trusts were unknown, while the "integration" phase of the combination movement could barely be discerned. Even the organization of credit and banking was still relatively crude, despite the very great progress achieved. And what can be said of countries like the states of Eastern Europe or even of Southern Europe which felt the influence of capitalism only by virtue of their relations with the outside world?

It should be remarked also that, around 1850, geographical concentration or localization of industry (*la concentration géographique*) was an accomplished fact, or nearly so, only in England. In no other country, also, was another of the most curious consequences of the progress of capitalism and large scale industry to be perceived, at least in equal degree. This is the growth of population, without which, according to Sombart, the full triumph of this capitalism would not have been possible.

Thus, the capitalistic régime has taken many centuries in its preparation; long embryonic, it has had a slow and painful adolescence. Even in the twentieth century, the transformation is far from fully achieved. This condition is doubtless one of the reasons which explain the structural strength of modern capitalism. The evolution has not been the result of artificial effort but the result of a variety of causes which have contributed to erect the capitalistic system. It is improbable, therefore, that social revolution, sudden and catastrophic in its workings, will be capable of overthrowing capitalism. This conclusion is contrary to that of Karl Marx in 1847, when he wrote the *Communist Manifesto;* but Karl Marx failed to probe to the deep seated foundations of modern capitalism.

CHAPTER X

SOCIAL REPERCUSSIONS

WOULD it not be fascinating to imagine precisely the various social repercussions of the economic movement which ended in the triumph of capitalism? Some phases of this problem are attacked in the present chapter; but necessarily a brief discussion must, by virtue of its brevity, concern itself only with the broader social relationships.

I. CAPITALISM AND SOCIAL UNREST IN THE MIDDLE AGES

Immediately upon its emergence during the Middle Ages, capitalism begins to engender social unrest. Especially is such the case in the Low Countries, as early as the thirteenth and fourteenth centuries. Thousands of workmen become economically dependent upon the merchants in the export industries (especially the cloth industry) who soon come into actual control of their output. From time to time these workers suffer the consequences of crisis and frequent unemployment, and while their employers are living on the fat of the land, they lead a very precarious existence. Moreover, the employers are well intrenched politically and control the city governments.

These conditions explain those uprisings of the "commoners" which broke out in the country round Liège and especially in the Flemish towns, as early as the thirteenth century. Such struggles were often violent, often bloody. The King of

France, who was allied to the urban patriciate, was defeated at Courtrai in 1302; but this defeat was revenged at Cassel, in 1328. The social struggles continued at the time of Artevelde, however; and, in the second half of the fourteenth century, came the new war with the King of France, which ended with his triumph at Roosebeke, in 1382, over the "horrible weavers."

But the urban patriciate was presently dislodged from control of the government in the Flemish towns, and the craftsmen took possession. Yet the governments which they set up, while democratic governments in fact, were very different from the ancient democracies, and very different from what we now understand a democracy to be. A guild spirit rather than a class spirit animated these craftsmen of the Middle Ages. But, while the guilds were used as the framework of the administrative life, the municipal governments were not transformed in any profound degree. The hated class of merchants, the *poorters*, still held their place in the political as well as the business life of the time. New political concepts emerged in the course of this social unsettlement.

In the Italian cities, analogous phenomena can be observed. There, too (notably in Florence), civil strife between social and economic classes developed into grave struggles between the "fat" and the "thin"—between the rich merchants and the body of the craftsmen. But these struggles failed to bring about radical transformation of the governmental institutions of the towns; indeed, the changes in Italy were far less sweeping even than those which occurred in the Low Countries. Neither does there seem to have been a class consciousness on the part of the landlords (*propriétaires*); and in the ranks of the Guelph and Ghibelline parties were to be found men of very different social extraction. And thus it is possible to explain, finally, how a "lord's party" (*parti du seigneur*), came to develop in many of these Italian republics, and in fact to

make the fortune of the *podestà*, of whom the Visconti represent the most significant type.[1]

Social unrest sometimes broke out in other countries at the
same period, though—since these countries had almost completely escaped from the influence of the building capitalism
—their troubles did not assume great proportions. The character of the Paris uprising in 1356, at the time of Etienne
Marcel, was entirely different from the troubles in the Flemish towns; on the other hand, the troubles caused by the *Maillotins* and the *Tuchins* were due mainly to social unrest,
though these were far more troubled and confused.[2]

II. INFLUENCE OF CAPITALISM ON LANDED PROPERTY AND THE AGRARIAN RÉGIME

(England, France, and the Baltic Countries)

What was the influence of the progress of capitalism on
the system of landed property, and consequently on the condition of the peasants in the different countries? From this
point of view, the experience of England seems particularly
instructive.[3] In that country, as everywhere else, the transition
from a natural economy (*Naturalwirtschaft*) to a money economy (*Geldwirtschaft*)—the consequence of the growth of
commerce—stimulated the substitution of money payments
for the customary labor of the manorial system. Consequently,
the change meant the freeing of the peasants from their customary obligations and the amelioration of their condition.

Then, in the fifteenth century, came the development of
the English woolen industry and the building up of the export trade in cloth. The demand for wool became greater and
greater, therefore, and sheep farming acquired a growing importance, especially in the southern and eastern counties.
The old forms of land tenure gave way to a system of farm
rents. Thus the old rural economy melted away in the face of

industrial progress. The rise of prices during the sixteenth century, which was felt in England as everywhere else in Western Europe, caused the lords to "round out" their nearby estates or *demesnes*, and to increase rents above the customary figures which their tenants had been paying. This movement accounts for the spread of enclosure, with the resultant evictions of numerous tenants. Properties were consolidated in the interest of the lords and greatly to the detriment of the small peasant proprietors, while the growth of sheep farming diminished the number of agricultural wage earners.[4]

Only in the eighteenth and nineteenth centuries does the practice of enclosure produce its full effect, however, and lead to the depopulation of the country and to the almost complete disappearance of "small holdings." Contrary to what has sometimes been said, the Industrial Revolution was not the essential cause of this great change; rather is the contrary the case, for the advent of large scale industry merely helped to complete the agrarian transformation, the more so because it affected the organization of manufacturing industry so profoundly. The rural and domestic industry (the "putting out" system of the countryside) gave way to the factory industry. Moreover, neither the elimination of the small peasant holdings nor the depopulation of the country districts took place everywhere with the same intensity: in Lancashire, for example, the change between 1740 and 1760 was quite gradual.[5]

The development of commercial capitalism also comes to exercise an important influence on the formation of the great landed estates. Many rich merchants acquire lands and seek to found "families" of gentlemen; and, as Daniel Defoe remarks: "after a generation or two, the tradesmen's children, or at least their grandchildren come to be as good Gentlemen, Statesmen, Parliament-men, Privy Counsellors, Judges, Bishops and Noblemen, as those of the highest birth and the most ancient families." [6] In France the sons of the newly rich seek appointments to public office, especially such offices as ensure the occupants a position in the nobility.

If the system of small peasant holdings, like the seigniorial régime, remained intact in France until the Revolution, the reason was in part that the effects of capitalism had permeated there much more slowly. In certain regions, to be sure, the inflow of specie during the sixteenth century and the progress of speculative activity had led to some concentration of landed properties and had produced a greater mobility and instability in the social state of the countryside. But in France nothing resembling the extraordinary development of the English woolen industry took place. Large scale maritime commerce never attained the same proportions in France as in England; and, in the seventeenth and eighteenth centuries, mobile capital failed to play anything like the rôle which it played in England. Nor were the effects of capitalism felt in the French countryside until the eighteenth century; and even the influence of capitalism was exerted only by the spread of the rural and domestic industry. No motive existed for substituting animal husbandry for agriculture, therefore, or for turning cultivated lands into pasturage. It is important to note, also, that the cultivators did not produce for export. The export of wheat was prohibited and freedom of export in the grain trade did not develop until the end of the *Ancien Régime*.

In France, therefore, the seigniorial system was preserved in its traditional form. The old agricultural methods persisted; and the seigneur, far from worrying about means to effect a concentration of his holdings, continued to divide his property among small or medium tenants (*métayers*) and share farmers. Not until the eighteenth century did the system of large scale farming begin to appear, notably in districts where agriculture had become prosperous, such as Beauce

and the north of France. The peasants continued to cultivate
small holdings and the division of the large properties went
on. The nobles, who often depended on the revenues of their
fiefs, had an interest in maintaining the integrity of the seigniorial régime. They were unwilling to attempt any measure
analogous to that of the English enclosures; nor were they in
position to carry through any such measure.

Another contribution of the progress of commercial capitalism seems to have been modification of the agrarian régime
in the Baltic countries. In these countries, the progress of capitalism increased the subjection of the peasants and reinforced
the position of the great noble proprietors. The countries
bordering on the Baltic (Poland, Latvia, Denmark, Russia)
were great producers of the cereals which the countries of
Southern Europe needed for their subsistence. In the seventeenth and eighteenth centuries, therefore, enormous quantities of grain were exported, through Stettin, then through
Hamburg, and later still through Danzig and Riga (all
towns situated at the mouth of navigable rivers), first by the
Hanseatic merchants, then by the Dutch. Though agriculture
was very much neglected in the Baltic countries, the nobles
managed to sell a great deal of wheat and rye abroad, at the
same time forcing the peasants to content themselves with
barley or oaten bread. Thus it was the export trade in wheat
which enabled the nobles to satisfy their desires for luxuries,
albeit at very high prices. Moreover, they had an interest in
increasing their properties; and control of an abundant labor
supply became more and more necessary for their farming
operations. As a consequence, serfdom took root in the Northeast of Europe, on the very eve of the emancipation of the
peasants in Western Europe. Thus it was, for example, that
during the sixteenth century, the Polish peasants who formerly had been free and subject only to quit-rents (*cens*), became, for the most part, serfs.

Such changes as went on in the Baltic countries were, however, the results of an influence brought to bear by capitalism only indirectly. Moreover, when capitalism did develop in the very regions where serfdom had been preserved, it stimulated the emancipation of the peasants. Serfdom tended to disappear because servile labor was found to be less productive than free labor. Indeed, a number of important Polish noblemen (*grands seigneurs*), both secular and ecclesiastical, made special concessions to German immigrants during the eighteenth century. These were made subject, not to labor dues, but to payments of quit-rents (*cens*); and they were allowed to enjoy personal liberty and a real local autonomy. It is a curious thing, indeed, that the great Polish nobles upheld the cause of enfranchising the serfs in the Diets of 1774, 1775, 1788, and 1791, while the minor lords, who depended upon labor dues, showed themselves hostile to the proposed reform.[7]

Then, of course, came the need for wage earners, as large scale industry began to develop. Such was notably the case in the Austro-Hungarian monarchy, where freedom from the last of the servile dues and manorial obligations came only after the Revolution of 1848. In Central Europe, moreover, the emancipation of the serfs did not reduce the extent of the noble properties; quite the contrary was the case, notably in Prussia where the change was favorable to the extension and the productivity of the large estates.[8]

The workings of the reaction of capitalism upon serfdom became much more apparent still in Russia, where the development of urban life, in the nineteenth century, accentuated the commercial character of agriculture. Efforts were made to bring about a more extensive system of agriculture, therefore; and the impossibility of increasing output, while at the same time preserving serfdom, was recognized, for serfdom prevents all agricultural progress. Thus it was the force of capitalism which brought about the emancipation of the Russian·serfs; the Crimean War—and the humanitarian campaign waged by the Russian writers—were only accidental causes. They merely hastened the Reform of 1861. Moreover, emancipation led to an increase in the supply of agricultural and industrial laborers. Consequently, it contributed to the progress of commercial and industrial capitalism in Russia, as elsewhere in Europe.

All the preceding discussion supports a fairly far-reaching conclusion, it seems to me. The condition of the peasants and, in a general way, the agrarian régime, resting on the solid base of the soil itself, tended to resist change; any internal tendency toward evolution made itself felt only very slowly. But pressure came from the outside—notably pressure derived from the commercial expansion and the workings of the money economy. This very general phenomenon, which has taken place at all times, may, in many respects, give the key which explains economic and social evolution. Local histories and regional monographs often furnish a concrete picture of the transition: here, for example, is the region of Rossendale, in the heart of Lancashire—a forest during the Middle Ages —which, in the eighteenth and nineteenth centuries becomes filled with the noise of factories and mills. And here, again, is an Alpine forest, long the seat of a peaceful pastoral life. In the present day mills, run by the electricity generated by "white coal" (the water power of the mountain stream), and railroads, which cross the mountains, are transforming it into a region of large scale industry. And, on the other hand, the valley of the Rhône—although a great commercial highway —waited until the nineteenth century to modify its traditional agricultural practices; for France (which, in the face of all, had continued to be essentially a country of peasants) had not yet changed her general economy in any profound fashion.

III. CAPITALISM AND THE ABOLITION OF SLAVERY

At first sight, it perhaps seems that the abolition of slavery was a product of the philanthropic sentiments and liberal ideas so strongly manifested during the French Revolution. Yet it appears also that the abolition movement was more or less directly related to the progress of capitalism. The influence of the principles of '89 is not to be denied, nor the action of certain English protestant sects. But did not the progress of large scale industry also demand the growth of a labor force freed from all servile obligations? Adam Smith in his *Wealth of Nations* had already made his opinion known:

> The experience of all ages and nations, I believe, demonstrates that the work done by slaves, although it appears to cost only their maintenance, is, in the end, the dearest of any. A person who can acquire no property can have no other interest but to eat as much and to labour as little as possible.

In the United States, moreover, it proved to be the trading and industrial states of the North which sustained the cause of emancipation. Following the victory of the North, industry began to develop in the old slave states. Moreover a good number of the writers who, before the war, came out in favor of emancipation of the blacks, had emphasized economic considerations. Such was the case with H. C. Carey, in his *Slave Trade, Domestic and Foreign* (1853), and Helper, in his *Impending Crisis*, written on the eve of the war between the States (1857). Both considered that progress in commerce and industry was incompatible with the maintenance of slavery. Yet the Southern States remained faithful to their old economic system, even when, toward the middle of the century, it had become clear that slave labor was not very remunerative, especially as the price of slaves continued to rise.

Southerners, to meet the threat which menaced them, must either have obtained the reëstablishment of the slave trade— a backward step quite out of the question since it was condemned by the opinion of all civilized peoples—or have opened up new and more fertile districts to slavery. On this account they sought to introduce slavery in the territories west of the Missouri. It was this effort which precipitated the American Civil War of 1861–1865.

Thus, while slavery and the slave trade had contributed to the building up of capitalism, it seems that the progress of capitalism was not without influence upon their abolition.

IV. INFLUENCE OF CAPITALISM ON THE TRANSFORMA-
TION OF THE LABORING AND MERCHANT CLASSES

The reaction of the different phases of the evolution of capitalism upon the condition of the merchant and laboring classes is even more readily apparent.

So long as commercial capitalism held sway, it was the merchant who played the outstanding rôle in economic life. The craftsmen and artisans of the countryside fell into a condition of economic dependence upon him, as did also a good number of the master workmen of the towns, at least in the textile industry. But the merchants paved the way for those masters and captains of industry who flourished in the period when capitalistic industry triumphed, though the latter (as Paul Mantoux rightly notes in his *Industrial Revolution*) were not "purely and simply the successors of the merchant-manufacturers of the eighteenth century." This historian makes the further shrewd observation that oftentimes members of the new class of business men did not resign themselves readily to changes in the practices which had been passed down from father to son. He notes also that many of the captains of industry were recruited from the country districts and, like the

Peels, from that class—half agricultural and half industrial —which has played such an important rôle in English economic and political life. The case of the iron masters appears to stand on a different basis, however, for in most cases, fathers and sons had specialized in the metal trades for generations.

In France, also, as Charles Ballot has shown, a good number of the industrial leaders of the early nineteenth century were "new men": such, for example, were Richard-Lenoir, the son of a farmer, and Oberkampf, son of a dyer. On the other hand, the case of François Perret may be cited; he was a manufacturer of silk goods from Lyons, who founded the great cotton establishment at Neuville in 1780. Moreover, at each phase in the evolution of capitalism—as Professor Pirenne has shown so well in his admirable memoir on the periods in the social history of capitalism (*Périodes de l'histoire sociale du capitalisme*)—the men who further the triumph of a new form of economic organization appear as self-made men. They are "upstarts," and *nouveaux riches*. Meanwhile, the representatives of the old order retire from the world of business, seeking quiet and aspiring only to join the ranks of the old aristocracy.[9] In England, it was their great ambition to enter the ranks of the landed gentry; and, once this had been achieved, they looked with scorn upon men of business. In France they sought to become public functionaries, and to fill offices which carried with them an *entrée* into the class of the nobility.

V. THE LABOR PROBLEM

When craftsmen fell under the economic domination of capitalistic *entrepreneurs*, notably in the textile industry, they contributed an important body to the wage-earning class. Many country workmen also joined the ranks of the urban

proletariat. The latter change came more slowly and less fever-
ishly in France than in England, because in France there was
never an enclosure movement, such as resulted in emptying
the English countryside. In France the small peasant holdings
have persisted.

In France, as in England, the development of large scale
capitalistic enterprise had the effect of raising a barrier, which
often proved insurmountable, between the class of the employers and the class of employees. Therefore, the working
class came to possess clearer consciousness of its collective interests, a development which was impossible when master and
journeyman led practically the same kind of life and when
there was no clean cut distinction between the different industrial classes. Under the new régime, the laborers were led
to organize for the defense of their *class interests*. This movement occurred much earlier in England than in France, because the industrial transformation was farther along there
and affected much denser masses of the population. The problem of the hour was to be no longer the *peasant problem* as in
1789; it was to be the problem of the industrial classes.

The employment of children and women in industry also
appears as one of the most striking social consequences of the
economic revolution. Children came to be employed much
earlier in England than on the Continent; and as early as 1802
the abuses had been so flagrant that a law was passed, regulating child labor. During the Napoleonic period, the employment of children (at first mainly wards of the government)
became general in the French cotton industry. The entrance
of women into manufacturing plants also came later in France
than in England. But in both countries, the mill-owners found
it to their interest to employ women and children, whose wages
were lower than those of men; thus their entrance into manufacturing industry was a direct consequence of the creation
of the large scale capitalistic industry.

The workers, on the whole, proved hostile to the industrial transformation and, above all, hostile to the introduction of machinery. In England this hostility was very strongly shown in the last twenty years of the eighteenth and the early years of the nineteenth century. Frequently the machines were broken up, and in 1811–1812 came the grave disorders of the Luddite movement. In France the process of evolution went at a slower pace than in England, and the incidental hardships proved less. In July 1789, the establishment of Brisout de Barneville at Rouen was destroyed in a popular outbreak; but under the First Empire no act of violence is recorded. Beginning with 1815, the demonstrations against machinery became more frequent, though they never assumed the same proportions as in England.

A very striking fact is that, before their own class movement took on a revolutionary aspect, it was the workmen, in the aggregate, who stood for the old order as against the new. They were the *conservatives*. Why this proved so, is readily understood; for the members of the working class were mainly thinking—and this very naturally—of the suffering which the innovations promised to inflict upon them. In England, they sought the maintenance and application of the old Elizabethan legislation, the regulations set up by the Statute of Artificers of 1563. They wished to have the apprenticeship requirement preserved, together with the limitation of the number of apprentices, and the fixing of wages by the Justices of the Peace. But their efforts failed and the *laissez-faire* principle triumphed over the principle of intervention; in 1813 and 1814 the regulations relating to wages and apprenticeship were abrogated. This repeal was achieved in the interest of the manufacturers, the new masters of industry who were straining every nerve to increase output. They proved to be the *innovators;* but hardly was their triumph achieved, before numerous thinkers undertook to criticise capitalistic society. At the same time the labor class organized to carry on the struggle against their employers.

There can be no doubt that large scale industrial operations aggravated the suffering of the working class, at least in the beginning. Yet it should not be forgotten that, even before the era of the factory—and in essentially agricultural countries, like Brittany—there was a laboring class much greater in number than has been ordinarily believed. The régime of small scale industry (*la petite industrie*) was no guaranty against misery. The guilds (even if it be admitted that they exercised a beneficent social influence) affected only a limited number of craftsmen, because many towns did not possess guild organizations. And even in towns where there were such, it was very rare that the majority of trades were so organized.

Even when consideration turns to England in the first half of the nineteenth century and to labor conditions there, it appears that, around 1839, workers in the English factory industries occupied a relatively favored position. Those in the worst positions were the workers in the knitting industry of Leicester, the silk weavers of Spitalfields, the woolen weavers of Yorkshire, the cotton weavers of Lancashire, and all household laborers. Their wages were an eighth of those of the mill workers, and they were able to hang on only because of the low wages which they accepted. These unhappy survivors of an outworn industrial régime were the real victims of large scale industrial operations and machinery, though the effects were brought about in an indirect manner. And it was they who contributed the principal strength to the Chartist movement, which, in the end, was forsaken by the labor organizations of the factory industries.[10] In France, at this same time, similar conditions obtained: thus Adolphe Blanqui notes that manufacturers with only crude equipment could compete with the better organized establishments only by reducing the wages of their workmen.

Care must be taken, however, lest the sufferings of the working class, in the aggregate, be underestimated. The echo of these sufferings is to be found not only in the poetic and vibrant *Past and Present* of Carlyle (1843) or the remarkable work which Friedrich Engels dedicated to the cause of the working class in England—*The Condition of the Working Classes in England in 1844* (1845), a work in which the revolutionary spirit of the author is often manifest—but in the marvelously balanced spirit of John Stuart Mill, whose *Principles of Political Economy* appeared three years later (1848) when revolution was disturbing the continent.

VI. CAPITALISM AND SOCIAL CLASSES. ECONOMIC DISTINCTIONS REPLACE LEGAL DISTINCTIONS

Another consequence of the triumph of capitalism has been that social classes have come to be based upon economic rather than legal distinctions. Quite the contrary was the case under the *Ancien Régime*. During the seventeenth and eighteenth centuries in France, distinctions between social classes were reinforced by distinctions of a legal or juridical nature. Thus the French nobility continued to recruit to some extent from the class of the wealthy, and especially from the world of finance; yet it also tended to become, in certain respects, a closed caste. The reformations of the nobility under Louis XIV (planned mainly as fiscal measures, to be sure) aimed at excluding families of recent extraction from the nobility; and they aimed especially at excluding magistrates of the lower courts, families which continued to engage in trade, and, finally, even gentlemen who were too poor to assert their rights. Thus, while parliamentary seats were closed to commoners in the eighteenth century, the nobility, on the other hand, had little choice other than to seek a military career. The barrier between nobles and commoners was raised higher and higher.

The effect of the Revolution was to destroy the legal distinctions which had divided the social classes and to establish equality of rights among all citizens. In 1789 the whole Third Estate had risen to demand the abolition of the privileges of the aristocracy, admission of all to all employments, and the overthrow of the seigniorial régime.

Without doubt, the economic changes of this period—the first "push" of capitalism—contributed greatly to the social transformation under way as 1789 drew near. The merchants (*négociants*) and men of business took an active part in the revolutionary events. This is a very significant fact which is only now being understood—an influence the importance of which new research may be expected to demonstrate.

It is also well to note that, so long as the social classes were distinguished mainly by their legal character, even the individuals who composed them had only a fairly confused notion of the social class to which they might belong. Thus, under the *Ancien Régime* the nobility comprised many different categories, both as regards the fortune and mode of living, and as regards privileges; and there were great differences between the nobility of the court and the country gentlemen, between the nobility of the sword and the nobility of the robe. To be sure, the noble was conscious that he belonged to a privileged caste, with relation to non-nobles, but he thought mainly of the *particular* privileges of the group to which he belonged; and, in the end, it was the *family interests* of the nobles which rested nearest their hearts. The nobles of the provincial Estates of Brittany were preoccupied mainly with the privileges of their group, as they constituted the most influential order in the assembly. Should a dispute arise with the royal government or its representatives, the nobility had a real chance of winning by joining efforts with the Parliament of Brittany, which—at least in the eighteenth century —was composed exclusively of nobles. No such alliance was ever made, however, and the Parliament on its part thought mainly of protecting its own particular interests. Here it was *esprit de corps* rather than class interest which was the controlling influence. In sum, the nobility had no clear concept of a collective interest before the Revolution, any more than did the other classes.

In 1789, when the privileged classes were forced to defend themselves against the claims of the Third Estate, their efforts were in the main exerted toward safeguarding a body of particular privileges; but this common effort was exerted without any real feeling of class solidarity. The non-privileged classes, on the contrary, realized that they all had the same claims to uphold, the same abuses to combat; and this realization led to the feeling—when they came to form a bloc against the nobility and clergy of the state—that they really represented the nation. But neither the middle class (*bourgeoisie*) nor even the peasants considered that they formed a very definite class. The *bourgeoisie* of the towns included many distinct groups; and in the country, there were well-to-do proprietors and small proprietors, farmers and share-tenants, and a class of property-less day laborers—quite different categories, whose interests often proved quite divergent. Thus it was that the well-to-do proprietors were opposed to the mass of peasants in the improvement of uncultivated lands. The peasants wished to preserve their rights in the commons, whereas it was to the interest of the proprietors to divide or even to appropriate such lands. The *Ancien Régime* was in fact a régime of antagonistic privileges; and this characteristic extended to all classes of society: nobility, *bourgeoisie*, and peasants alike.

Once the Revolution had been launched, the conflicting interests of the several classes which made up the Third Estate became more apparent. On the one hand, there were the rich *bourgeoisie* and, on the other, the groups of the Third Estate, which suffered acutely from the depreciation of the *assignats*, and from the high cost of living—the small shopkeepers and petty tradespeople (*le petit bourgeois*), the artisans, and the laboring class. It was from the latter groups that the *sans culottes* were recruited; and upon them the radical government (*Montagnard*) leaned during the Terror. It is clear, therefore, not only that the Third Estate (which constituted a class in the legal sense) did not form a *bloc*, but also that its several elements tended to pull apart in the course of the Revolution.

In the nineteenth century, on the contrary, the notion of social classes and a consciousness of class interests grew; and the idea of a class struggle received more and more acceptance. One of the great reasons for this development (others there are, of course) was that the abolition of juridical or legal classes and the progress of capitalism had brought about a new distribution of the social classes, a distribution based on the rôle played in economic life. The class of big business men, those engaged in commerce, as well as the heads of large scale industrial plants, took on increasing importance. The barriers between employers and the workmen whom they employed became more difficult to surmount. It was under such circumstances—and in response to such influences—that the working class then really originated, and began to feel conscious of its collective or class interests.

In present day society, therefore, class distinctions are essentially of an economic nature. And entrance into the directing class, the capitalistic class—largely composed of new and self-made men—is open to those with the essential personal qualities. Thus, the new concept of social classes has come to be very closely connected with the individualistic organization of society. Today, an individual is attached much less closely than heretofore to the social group of which he is a part. No doubt, from the economic point of view, he has class interests; but in every other domain of life (the intellectual and political, for example) he is free to attach himself to other groups. Thus, social mobility appears much greater in the present day than it used to be; and our highly individualistic society forms a most striking contrast with the rigid caste system of India.

At the same time, as has been justly remarked, the division of labor is becoming greater and greater in present day society. Whether in the field of administration or of politics, the tendency toward greater specialization is being steadily accentuated. New trades, new industries, or new accessory trades are constantly created; and this phenomenon has the effect, moreover, (as Eduard Bernstein has noted) of delaying economic concentration. This is why the craftsmen who make up the artisan class have not entirely disappeared, although their importance is growing steadily less. Yet, however great the progress of capitalism, its triumph has by no means been so complete as Karl Marx had imagined. Many characteristics of the old organization of labor persist, even in the countries where the evolution of capitalism has gone the farthest.

This is but one of the qualifications of the Marxian philosophy which must be made. Others are revealed by study of the facts of present day economic life. If the working class today possesses a clearer consciousness of its collective interests—in large part, the consequence of the influences making for concentration of industrial life—yet this class consciousness has not asserted itself either as rapidly or as completely as the Marxian doctrine contemplated. As early as 1839, for example, the English trade unions had ceased to be interested in Chartism. The point of view that there was not a class solidarity even in the working classes was stated by one of the delegates at the Birmingham meeting of Chartists when he pointed out that Chartism could obtain unanimity only in the ranks of the poorest paid. Men who earned 30 shillings a week would not concern themselves with those who earned 15, and the latter cared equally little for those earning 5 or 6 shillings. Was there not a working-class aristocracy, as well as one in the *bourgeois* world? After all, the Chartist movement (which, in M. Halévy's phrase, was only "a hunger revolt") did not proceed from socialistic premises.[11]

In England, where the changes which constitute the Industrial Revolution first took place and were most intense, the transition period had been accompanied by grave social troubles. And yet the flowering of the socialistic doctrines in the first half of the nineteenth century was much less vigorous there than in France, where industrial capitalism manifested itself later and much less intensely. The persistent agitation on social questions in France seems, in certain degree, to have been a continuation of the remarkable growth of French ideas which characterized the eighteenth century. It is also most interesting to observe that, in France, the socialistic propaganda of the middle of the nineteenth century was mainly successful among the Parisian workmen, such as the workers in small industries and workers in small plants and the luxury industries, whose condition had hardly changed since the days of the *Ancien Régime*. Workers in the modern large scale industry (*la grande industrie*), on the other hand, showed themselves far more unsympathetic to the new doctrines.

Thus the social repercussions of capitalism cannot be represented by any such definite formulae as Marxian orthodoxy would have us believe. We must allow for the influence of ideas, and not accept literally the materialistic concept of history. If the triumph of capitalism has made possible the constitution of class parties, such as the socialist parties, yet the influence of theorists and in particular of Karl Marx, has had some part—even an important part—in the class movement; for they have contributed largely to the awakening of class consciousness in the proletariat. Yet this awakening of a class consciousness has been no sudden development: though still obscure in the eighteenth century, it has slowly emerged from the domain of the subconscious. Here again we perceive the effects of a slow evolution, determined by complex phenomena, such as one is oftentimes tempted to simplify excessively.[12]

CHAPTER XI

CONCLUSION

I

THE discussion of the preceding chapters points very clearly to one important conclusion; namely, that, though the accumulation of capital is a necessary condition for the creation of a capitalistic society, the mere existence of capital is not enough to create such a society.

A further conclusion which stands out in clear focus is that capital was accumulated mainly through the agency of commerce and particularly through commercial operations when carried forward on a large scale. Following the Crusades, trade with the Orient unloosed a stream of wealth toward the Western World, a stream which resulted in a capital accumulation of quite considerable proportions. The great Italian cities profited most from this trade; and this is why the first signs of a capitalistic organization appeared in the city-republics of the Italian peninsula.

But Italy could not keep this wealth for herself alone; and an international current of exchanges was established, notably toward the northwest of Europe. The effects of this new economic stimulus were soon felt in the Low Countries; and at an early date, therefore, evidence of a "nascent capitalism" appeared there. Quite naturally, also, strategic points on the principal trade routes of the time were marked by the great fairs, of which those of Champagne may be taken as typical. At first, in these fairs, the objects of exchange were goods and merchandise of various kinds. But only in quite primitive times was simple barter a satisfactory basis of trading; and a system of purchase and sale necessitated the use of money. Next the great variety of coins led to the development of a special group of merchants and traders, who undertook the function of money changing. Out of their operations, in turn, came the beginnings of foreign exchange as we know it today. Its early form, the bill of exchange was the *lettre de foire;* but presently the modern bill of exchange was developed since it was necessary to provide not only for immediate settlements of accounts in cash, but also for settlements after a period of time had elapsed. Still more important, as Paul Huvelin has shown so well, was the development of a system for the cancelling of debts by the device of transferring and cancelling such bills of exchange as fell due at the fairs. This device (*virements de partie* or *scontration*) was a sort of clearing house operation.

Thus, commercial capitalism necessarily gave rise to financial capitalism; and this, in turn, contributed to the further accumulation of capital, by bringing about a more active circulation of goods and wealth. Then another element came into play, an element which Werner Sombart has brought to light very well: the great princely or monarchical states found their needs for money constantly increasing. Their borrowings enriched all who engaged in the money trade: tax collectors, lenders, and bankers alike. The birth of public credit seems to have contributed strongly to the development of the great financial houses, which appeared at the dawn of modern times.

Another manifestation of the evolution of capitalism was the creation of *bourses*. From the sixteenth century onward, these assumed a growing importance; and gradually they came to supplant the great fairs. Whereas the several operations of purchase, sale, and settlement had been only intermittent or periodic in the case of the fairs, they became matters of daily routine once the *bourses* were functioning. It can be readily understood, therefore, how greatly the invention of the *bourse* contributed to the progress of capitalism.

The importance of exchange operations, and their steady increase soon obliged governments, if not the Church, to recognize the legitimacy of lending at interest—and lending at interest is, again, one of the essential foundation stones of modern capitalism. Then the transactions to which exchange operations gave rise in different places, with *rates* fixed in the fairs and the *bourses*, had the further result of bringing negotiable securities into general use. This development in turn brought a greater and greater mobility to economic affairs. Trading operations came to be less and less an exchange of actual merchandise than an exchange of the *abstract* representations of such goods as were evidenced by the corresponding papers or documents. This further development explains the constantly growing importance of speculative operations and even of gambling. Speculation had previously attained considerable proportions, notably at Antwerp in the sixteenth century, where capitalism had been allowed to run its course without restraint! Was not Antwerp the seat of "unbridled capitalism?"

II

Yet Antwerp was still but an islet in a society founded mainly on landed property, and the interests concerned therewith; and even at Antwerp, the financial dealings were in figures which today would seem almost ridiculously small.

A new inflow of wealth and capital was necessary; and this came as the consequence of the great discoveries, and the seizure of the New World by the powers of Western Europe. Beginning with the sixteenth century, maritime and colonial commerce threw an enormous mass of wealth onto the markets of Europe. Included were the precious wares of the tropics, of the Far East, and especially gold and silver from the New World. Another point of great importance is that this maritime and colonial commerce led to the creation of the first great trading corporations. Such companies—notably the English and Dutch East India Companies—gave a fillip to capitalism and provided powerful machinery suitable for vigorous action in developing new markets and new sources of supply.

Thus it appears that capitalism first developed in its commercial form and then in its financial form. And, without doubt, such was, in fact, its origin. The essential characteristic distinguishing a capitalistic regime from other economic systems is the mobility of capital, which in degree overcomes the obstacles born of time and distance. And presently, capital (accumulated with a view of obtaining an income) sets claim to a remuneration which is no longer the actual reward of labor alone. Recognition is afforded a *time* function in economic life; and a practice arises which runs contrary to the concepts of antiquity and of the Middle Ages—the payment of interest. This even runs counter to the doctrines of the Church, which had followed Aristotle in refusing to admit that money might breed money.

Then, in the seventeenth century, came the rise of Holland as a great economic power. Her strength depended entirely on commercial and financial capitalism, and her supremacy was mainly the result of her success in maritime commerce and in the traffic in negotiable securities. But her decline is presaged by the beginning of the eighteenth century; for, of necessity, Holland was a commercial, not an industrial, country. England and, in a certain measure, France, therefore usurped her place, because their exports were not limited to the products of agriculture alone but included also goods produced by manufacturing industry. The decline of Holland and the rise of England and France therefore mark the moment when commercial and financial capitalism begins to extend its sway over manufacturing industry.

III

This change marks the beginning of a revolution in the organization of industry, for manufacturing had long been in the hands of petty tradesmen possessing little, if any, capital. Manufacturing is gradually transformed into a great capitalistic industry. The first stage of this evolution is marked by the supremacy of merchant business men (*marchands-entrepreneurs*) whose efforts to increase their own profits led to efforts to control the rural and domestic industry. The craftsman in the countryside or the master silk workman of Lyons no longer maintained direct relations with his customers; it was the master-merchant who sought out distant markets and guided and "controlled" production. And to this specialized business man or man of affairs—and no longer to the craftsman—went the larger part of the profits.

Next this business man is transformed into a captain of industry. The forces making for a concentration of labor and machinery in a factory, as well as the machine process itself, had already reduced the workers to the condition of ordinary wage earners. Finally, industrial capitalism truly triumphs, when corporations—which at first had appeared only in a few industries where the equipment was particularly costly (mining enterprises, for example)—spread to all branches of manufacturing enterprise. But final victory must await improvement in the organization of credit and banking and still another new development: the revolution in the means of communication and transportation, made possible by the steam engine.

But, however great the importance of commercial capitalism, the rôle of industry cannot be disregarded. Was it not the progress of the woolen industry which stimulated the great export movement from England in the fifteenth century? And, in modern times, industrial production has become still more a necessary support of commercial and financial activity. Indeed, this is one of the reasons why England has outdistanced Holland.

In a word, the essential characteristic of present day capitalistic society is that all three forms of capitalism—commercial capitalism, financial capitalism, industrial capitalism—now function concurrently. The latest to develop—the industrial form—has so greatly eclipsed the other two, in externals at least, that it has often been considered—*wrongly, however*—as the essential manifestation of capitalism. To be sure, modern capitalism has gradually spread over a great share of productive enterprise. Yet there are some regions and some industries which are still pretty much unaffected by it. Even in the regions where capitalistic enterprise is most widespread, small scale industry has not disappeared and craftsmen still persist. Men, and particularly women, continue to work at home, principally in such finishing and fitting operations as those necessary in the making of ready-made clothing. And how many countries there are where the influence of capitalism is only now beginning to filter in or where contact with capitalism is now limited solely to dealings with the outside world!

It must not be forgotten, furthermore, that agriculture has escaped the influence of capitalism in very large measure. Agriculture has doubtless been subject to the influence of capitalism from an early date; but agriculture is of necessity fixed to the soil (the stable element *par excellence*), and it is even today affected by capitalism only to the extent that it must reckon with commercial speculation or with credit in its general forms. Moreover, this "conservative" character of agriculture is especially true of old Europe; in new countries, like the United States, agricultural enterprise does assume a more capitalistic character. There the farmer tends to be something of a business man.

In the course of modern times, the influence of capitalism has gradually spread over more and more branches of economic effort; and since the end of the eighteenth century, it has spread steadily over new areas. Thus a critical moment arrived when the influence of capitalism was felt in the New World; and, in this respect, the breaking down of the colonial system had an immense effect. In the beginning the colonial system contributed powerfully to the development of capitalism, and it is one of the ironies of history that the development of capitalism in turn brought about the overturn of the trade monopolies set up in the interest of the mother country. Such monopolies were presently to be recognized as increasingly troublesome hindrances to all economic expansion. Therefore, the downfall of the colonial system can be traced directly to the advent of industrial capitalism.

IV

In order to understand the nature of present day capitalism, the evolutionary process, by which it came into being, must be understood. Certainly to study capitalism only as a function of labor is not enough. This is what Karl Marx did. Above all, the primordial elements in the growth of capitalism —its commercial form and its financial form—should not be lost sight of—for, in the end, these emerge as the most important. The concept of *product without labor*, which Marx rightly calls the most characteristic aspect of the capitalistic régime, is even more vividly explained if the mechanism of the exchanges is taken into account. These led to other forms of speculation. Another important relationship is that which exists between capitalism and the idea of gambling, of risk assumption. This relationship is involved in future transactions in negotiable securities, and also in the several varieties of insurance, of which the *grosse aventure* seems to have been the earliest form.[1]

Karl Marx had also the great merit of describing, more clearly than had been done before him, the social repercussions which came out of the evolution of capitalism. Furthermore, he showed that the triumph of capitalism had as a consequence the creation of social classes, distinguished by economic rather than legal and juridical distinctions. This change has had the effect of making society infinitely more mobile and active, and at the same time more unstable. But Karl Marx based his doctrine mainly on contemporaneous facts. To understand social transformations in all their complexity, we must envisage the historical evolution in all its ramifications and must study the first symptoms of the new organization. Only by attentive and infinitely minute study of historical data, and by avoiding all *a priori* notions, all political and social prejudices, can we form a fairer idea of the origins of modern capitalism and of the true character of the economic and social organization which determined it, and which is now manifest in its full flowering.

Study of such facts makes clear that class consciousness in the laboring class did not manifest itself as suddenly as has often been pretended and that it did not proceed solely from economic transformations. The influence of ideas must be taken into account.

v

There is another series of questions which have been only touched upon here. What, for example, has been the reaction of the increasing influence of capitalism on other phenomena

of a political, intellectual, or religious character? And what
has been the reaction of the latter on the new form of economic organization?

The pressure of capitalism, as it first manifested itself in
the Middle Ages, notably in Italy and in the Low Countries,
helped to dissolve the old feudal system. This is clearly seen
in the Italian republics and especially at Florence. From the
beginning of modern times, also, the progress of the princely
and monarchical states has contributed in marked degree to
the formation of great financial houses, of which the Fuggers
are the most striking type. The borrowings of sovereigns
served to increase greatly the importance of the trade and
speculation in loans. On the other hand, the absolute monarchies, by creating strong unified states on the ruins of the
feudal powers, enlarged the field of action open to the commercial and financial forces.

If capitalism be held responsible for much suffering—perhaps rather more during the long period of its elaboration
than in the time of its full flowering—it must be recognized
also as a powerful instrument for intellectual activity and
emancipation. This is doubtless the great reason why Italy, by
the fourteenth century, and the Low Countries at the dawn
of modern times, were the seats of activity in science, in letters, and in art—indeed the reason why the Renaissance was
there particularly flourishing and fruitful.[2] The creation of
great personal fortunes produced an entire class of enlight-
ened patrons of the arts and letters. The whole history of
the fine arts bears witness to this, especially with respect to
Italy and the Low Countries.[3] It is also very significant that
in the seventeenth century Holland produced both a Rem-
brandt, and a Ruysdaël. Holland was then a center of scientific activity as well as a seat of intellectual liberty, the asylum
and refuge of thinking men.

A connection can even be traced between the evolution of

capitalism and the religious movements. The Church frowned upon the "money trade" and stood out tenaciously against loans at interest and against speculation on the exchanges and in securities. On the other hand, the individualism manifest in the economic life in the sixteenth century also found expression in the field of religion; it was expressed in the protests which led to the Reformation, and principally in Calvinism. Calvin upheld the legitimacy of loans at interest; and the Non-Conformists contributed greatly toward the accumulation of capital. In the latter respect, also, the influence of the Jews is undeniable, although it should not be exaggerated.

Finally, connections, often fairly close, can be traced between the evolution of capitalism and other forms of historical evolution. But it is often difficult to disentangle the reciprocal influences and to distinguish causes from effects— for these evolutionary developments are very complex phenomena. Yet it has been worth while to indicate even some of the unsolved problems, since the clear statement of such questions may well serve to open fruitful paths of investigation and stimulate new researches.

NOTES

CHAPTER I

[1] In France the word "capital" was at first only an adjective. The present day meaning of *capital* was expressed, in the seventeenth century, by the word *principal*, or by the word *interest*. For example, such an expression as the following was used: "to take an interest of 5000 *livres* in a business." Only in the course of the eighteenth century did the word capital really begin to take on its present meaning. Profits accruing in commerical joint stock companies were described by the word *bénéfice* and not by the word *interest*. This latter word, in the modern sense, seems to have appeared only very late, just at the period when corporations were developing. See H. Sée, *L'évolution du sens des mots intérêt et capital* (*Revue d'histoire économique*, 1924). In England the word *stock* was first used, then the term *capital* stock; see E. Cannan, *A History of the Theories of Production and Distribution in English Political Economy*, 3rd ed., London, 1924. However, the word *capital* had been used, as early as the sixteenth century, in treatises on accounting, one French and several English, which seem to be inspired by Italian works of the same nature. See the very interesting article by R. D. Richards, *Early History of the Term Capital* (*The Quarterly Journal of Economics*, Vol. XL, p. 329 *et seq.*), and Henry Rand Hatfield, *Earliest Use in English of the Term Capital* (*Ibid.*, p. 547).

CHAPTER II

[1] The functions performed by the Roman bankers *(argentarii)* are discussed by William Stearns Davis, *The Influence of Wealth in Imperial Rome*, New York, 1910, p. 73–79.

[2] See, on this subject, the remarkable study of Max Weber, in his *Gesammelte Aufsätze zur Sozial- und Wirtschaftsgeschichte*, Tübingen, 1924.

[3] See Joseph Calmette, *Le régime féodal*, Armand Colin Collection, Paris, 1923; also the delightful volume by Professor William Stearns Davis, *Life on a Medieval Barony, A Picture of a Typical Feudal Community*, New York, 1923.

[4] For a brief and clear discussion of the manorial system, see Melvin M. Knight, *Economic History of Europe*, Boston, 1926, p. 162–198. The various manorial obligations are explained at p. 176–177.

[5] To a considerable extent the prosperity of the German towns of the West and South was due to their relations with the countries of the Mediterranean. *Cf.* Alays Schulte, *Geschichte des Mittelalterlichen Handels und Verkehrs zwischen Westdeutschland und Italien* (2 vols.), Leipzig, 1900.

[6] The Cahorsins, natives of the city of Cahors, now the capital of the French department of Lot, carried on a trade in money much like that carried on by the Jews.

[7] See Camille Piton, *Les Lombards en France et à Paris*, Paris, 1892; Werner Sombart (*Der Bourgeois*, Leipzig, 1913, translated into English by M. Epstein under the title *Quintessence of Capitalism*, London, 1915) seeks to show that it was the Italians who first showed "the capitalist mentality" and the "*bourgeois* ideal" which emphasize the virtues of activity, exactness, and especial care in the accurate keeping of accounts. His principal source is the work of L. B. Alberti, *Libri della famiglia*, Florence, 1908.

[8] On the economic progress of northwest of Europe, after the tenth century, *cf.* also Paul Kletler, *Nordwesteuropa's Verkehr, Handel, und Gewerbe*, Vienna, 1924. (Collection *Deutschekultur*.)

[9] In Ghent, for example, there were 4,000 such workmen out of a total population of 50,000 inhabitants.

[10] G. des Marez shows this in his *Etude sur la propriété foncière dans les villes au moyen âge*, Ghent, 1898.

[11] See J. G. van Dillen, *Het economisch karakter der middeleeuwsche stad*, Amsterdam, 1914; H. J. Smit, *De Opkomst van den handel van Amsterdam*, Amsterdam, 1914; Z. W. Sneller, *Le développement du commerce entre les Pays-Bas septentrionaux et la France jusqu'au milieu du XVe siècle* (*Revue du Nord*, 1922). It should be noted furthermore that, beginning with the Middle Ages, a considerable textile industry developed in the Northern Low Countries. N. W. Posthumus, *De Geschiedenis van de Leidsche laken industrie*, The Hague, 1908.

[12] H. E. de Sagher, *Les immigrations de tisserands flamands et brabançons en Angleterre sous Edward III*, in the *Mélanges Pirenne*, Brussels, 1926, p. 109, shows that the influence of these immigrants upon the development of the textile industry has been exaggerated.

[13] See Ramón Carande, *Sevilla fortaleza y mercado* (*Anuario de historia del derecho español*, vol. II, 1925).

[14] The *lettre de foire* seems to have been the first form of the bill of exchange. One merchant delivered the bill to another, to be receipted at a designated fair. The *lettre de foire* did not attain the mobility of the bill of exchange. See G. des Marez, *La lettre de foire à Ypres au XIII° siècle*, Brussels, 1901.

[15] At Genoa, by the twelfth century, the "sea loan" had developed in maritime commerce. This was a method of insuring against the risks of the sea without violating the prohibitions against usury. The sea loan finally took the form of "the loan at great risk," a form which persisted, especially when sea voyages to distant parts were undertaken. When certain risky maritime ventures were to be undertaken, a certain sum, for example 10,000 *livres*, was obtained for the cargo belonging to such and such a person or capitalist. If the ship was lost, no repayment was exacted by the lender; if it reached port safely, the borrower paid a considerable premium, sometimes fifty per cent. Thus the sea loan had a fairly close connection with maritime insurance, properly so called. See the excellent article by Calvin B. Hoover, *The Sea Loan in Genoa in the Twelfth Century;* in *The Quarterly Journal of Economics*, vol. XL, p. 495 *et seq.*

[16] This has been shown by Josef Kulischer in his study *Warenhändler und Geldausleiher im Mittelalter (Zeitschrift für Volkswirtschaft, Sozialpolitik und Verwaltung*, vol. XVII). Other discussions of the economic rôle of the Jews in the Middle Ages are: Moses Hoffmann, *Der Geldhandel der deutschen Juden während des Mittelalters, bis zum Jahre 1350*, Leipzig, 1910; Georg Caro, *Sozial- und Wirtschaftsgeschichte der Juden*, vol. I, Leipzig, 1908; B. Hahn, *Die Wirtschaftliche Tätigkeit der Juden im frankischen und deutschen Reich bis zum zweiten Kreuzzug*, Freiburg, 1911; M. Kayserling, *Geschichte der Juden im Portugal*, Leipzig, 1867.

[17] Notably by means of numerous purchases of ground rents; in the thirteenth century, the abbeys of Normandy played the part of agricultural banks. See R. Génestal, *Rôle des monastères comme établissements de crédit, étudié en Normandie du XI° à la fin du*

XIII siècle*, Paris, 1901; and also Georges Mayer, *Essai sur les origines du crédit en France du XI* à la fin du XIII* siècle*, Paris, 1902.

[18] See Léopold Delisle, *Les opérations financières des Templiers* (*Mém. de l'Académie des Inscriptions*, vol. 33, 1889); H. Prutz, *Entwickelung und Untergang des Tempelherrenordens*, Berlin, 1888; and on all that precedes, see the excellent study of Josef Kulischer, *op. cit.*

[19] See Werner Sombart, *Der moderne Kapitalismus*, 4th ed., Munich, 1921; on the criticism of Sombart's theory of capitalism in the Middle Ages, see G. von Below, *Die Entstehung des modernen Kapitalismus* (*Historische Zeitschrift*, 1903, vol. 91); and L. Brentano, *Die Anfänge des modernen Kapitalismus*, Munich, 1916.

CHAPTER III

[1] In his celebrated work, *Die Entstehung der Volkswirtschaft*, Tübingen, 1893; translated by S. M. Wickett under the title *Industrial Evolution*, New York, 1901.

[2] *Studien zur Geschichte kapitalistischer Organisationsformen*, Munich and Leipzig, 1914. Strieder also shows that, by this time, numerous "monopolies" were being set up. But is it not something of an anachronism to entitle understandings among merchants "cartels"? See also his *Jacob Fugger der Reiche*, Leipzig, 1926.

[3] On all the foregoing, see Werner Sombart, *Der moderne Kapitalismus*, Part II, Chapters 10 and 11, Leipzig, 1902; 2nd ed., 1916–17.

[4] Henri Pirenne shows this in his *Les périodes de l'histoire sociale du capitalisme* (*Mémoires de l'Académie de Belgique*), Brussels, 1914.

[5] On this question, see André Allix, *Les Foires* (*La Géographie*, 1923). However, the regional fairs—at least in France—continued to retain a notable commercial importance until the nineteenth century; see H. Sée, *Notes sur les foires en France et particulièrement sur les foires de Caen au XVIIIᵉ siècle* (*Revue d'histoire économique*, 1927).

[6] "Dry Exchange" is discussed at length in the introduction to Thomas Wilson's *A Discourse upon Usury*, edited by R. H. Tawney, London, 1925, p. 73–77, where (p. 75) "Dry Exchange" is defined as "nothing more mysterious than what would today be called a finance bill," and in the *Discourse* p. 305–309, where the "kynde of billes or

,merchandising exchange . . . called secke and drye exchange" are discussed.

[7] See the excellent work of R. H. Tawney, *Religion and the Rise of Capitalism*, London, 1926; H. Hauser, *A propos des idées économiques de Calvin* (*Mélanges Pirenne*, Brussels, 1926); H. Sée, *Dans quelle mesure Puritains et Juifs ont-ils contribué aux progrès du capitalisme?* (*Revue historique*, May 1927), reprinted in *Science et philosophie de l'histoire*, Paris, 1928.

[8] In his fine work, *Das Zeitalter der Fugger* (Jena, 1896). An interesting collection of Fugger papers has been published under the title *The Fugger News Letters*, 1568–1605, edited by Victor von Klarwill, New York, 1924. *Second series*, 1926.

[9] As early as the sixteenth century there was what was in fact a *bourse* at Amsterdam, although it did not yet have a building of its own. The building was not erected until 1611. The economic development of Amsterdam further increased the importance of this *bourse* in the seventeenth century. Moreover, the *bourse* where trading in goods was carried on (the *bourse de marchandises*) gradually became also a stock exchange, at least towards the end of the century. See the very interesting article by J. G. van Dillen, *Termijnhandel te Amsterdam in de 16de en 17de eeuw* (in *De Economist*, 1927).

[10] There were also Swiss and Spanish banks; and bankers from Lyons were numerous elsewhere in Europe as early as the sixteenth century.

CHAPTER IV

[1] See Werner Sombart, *op. cit.*, Chap. XIII; Oscar Peschel, *Geschichte des Zeitalter der Entdeckungen*, Stuttgart, 1877. On the other hand, once the period of brutal conquest was ended, the Spanish colonists often made praiseworthy efforts to improve the immense continent of which they had taken possession; the great scholar Humbolt recognizes this. *Cf.* C. Pereyra, *La obra de España en América*, Madrid, 1920, translated into French: *L'œuvre de l'Espagne en Amérique*, Paris, 1925; and also J. B. Teran, *El nacimiento de la América española*, Tucuman, 1927.

[2] See Werner Sombart, *Die Juden und der Wirtschaftsleben*, Leipzig, 1911; translated into English (by M. E. Epstein): *The Jews*

and Modern Capitalism, London, 1913; and Goris, *Les colonies mar-chandes méridionales à Anvers de 1488 à 1565*, Louvain, 1925. Unfortunately, we have but few works on the economic and commercial activities of the Portuguese.

[3] The production of gold increased only fairly slightly (by about a sixth). *Cf.* Adolph Soetbeer, *Materialien zur Erläuterung und Beurteilung der wirtschaftlichen Edelmetallverhältnisse und der Wahrungsfrage*, Berlin, 1885; a translation in English by Professor F. W. Taussig appeared in a special report (*Bimetallism in Europe*), December 1887, of the United States *Consular Reports*.

[4] Jean Bodin shows this in his famous *Résponse aux paradoxes de M. de Malestroit touchant l'enchérissement de toutes les choses et des monnaies*, Paris, 1568.

[5] This was shown recently by Paul Raveau in his fine study which appears in *L'agriculture et les classes paysannes dans le Haut-Poitou au XVI° siècle, op. cit.*

[6] See Henri Hauser, *Controverse sur les monnaies* (*Travailleurs et marchands de l'ancienne France*, Paris, 1920). The influx of the precious metals was not, however, the sole cause of the rise of prices. Beginning with 1570, and continuing until the end of the century, the ravages produced by the wars of religion must be taken into account. *Cf.* Liautey, *La hausse des prix et la lutte contra la cherté en France au XVI° siècle*, Paris, 1921, and Paul Harsin, *L'afflux des métaux précieux au XVI° siècle et la théorie de la monnaie chez les auteurs français* (*Revue d'histoire économique*, 1927, No. 3).

[7] This memoir was uncovered in the Bibliothèque Nationale at Paris by P. J. Blok in 1896, and was published by him with a brief introduction at The Hague in 1898 under the title *Een merkwaardig aanvalsplan gericht tegen visscherij en handel der Vereeinigde Nederlanden in de eerste helft der 17de eeuw*. The passage quoted above appears at p. 17 of this reprint, a copy of which is in the Harvard College Library.

[8] See William Cunningham, *The Growth of English Industry and Commerce, Modern Times*, 3rd ed., 1903, p. 1 *et seq.*, 63 *et seq.* See also Professor Edward Channing, Chapter V, in vol. I of his *History of the United States*, "The English Seamen," a brief and entertaining account of Hawkins and Drake and their exploits, New York, 1907.

[9] *Ibid.*, p. 218 *et seq.* According to George Unwin, in his article,

Merchant Adventurers under the Reign of Elizabeth (in the *Economic History Review*, 1926 and reprinted in *Studies in Economic History*, London, 1927), this Company hindered the commercial and industrial progress of England.

[10] See W. R. Scott, *Joint Stock Companies to 1720*, vol. I, Cambridge, 1910–12, p. 78 *et seq.* The story is dramatically told by Professor Channing, *The History of the United States*, 1907–.

[11] To be sure, there had been *societates* in Italy, as early as the Middle Ages. These had two forms: in one of these, all the associates took part in the management; whereas, the other, called the *commenda*, resembled the limited partnerships which are found in England today. Professor Jakob Strieder (*Studien zur Geschichte kapitalistischer Organisationsformen*, 2nd ed.) has shown that there were joint stock companies in Germany around the beginning of the sixteenth century, notably in mining. But for the most part these were family affairs and in any case the shares did not possess the mobility to transfer which distinguished the shares of the Dutch East India Company.

CHAPTER V

[1] See C. H. Haring, *Trade and Navigation between Spain and the Indies in the time of the Hapsburgs* (Harvard economic studies), Cambridge, 1918, p. 111 *et seq.*, and *The Buccaneers in the West Indies in the XVIIth Century*, London, 1910.

[2] See E. W. Dahlgren, *Les relations commerciales et maritimes entre la France et les côtes de l'océan Pacifique*, Paris, 1909; Léon Vignols, *Le commerce interlope français à la mer du Sud (Revue d'histoire économique*, 1925). After 1724, the contraband commerce of the French, forbidden by their government, ceased almost completely; cf. H. Sée and L. Vignols, *La fin du commerce interlope (Ibid.*, 1925).

[3] In 1713 Spain by agreement (*asiento*) had conceded to France the privilege of carrying negro slaves to the Spanish colonies. This privilege France surrendered by the Treaty of Utrecht; and by the Treaty *de l'Asiento* it was granted to England for 33 years from May 1, 1713. England engaged to furnish 4,800 slaves annually and in return was entitled to send two ships every year with negroes for America. At the outbreak of war with Spain, the *Asiento* was suspended, but it was renewed in 1725 and again in 1748. The principal

provisions appear in Hosack's *Law of Nations*, p. 355, London, 1882. *Cf.* Georges Scelle, *La traite négrière aux Indes de Castille*, Paris, 1904; Vera L. Brown, *The Contraband Trade* (*American Historical Review*, 1926); R. F. Lavene, *Comercio de Indias*, Buenos Aires, 1916.

⁴ Published in 1664; available in the *Reprints of Economic History Classics*, (Publication of the Economic History Society), Oxford, 1927.

⁵ A curious anonymous pamphlet of 1698 attributes these speculative operations mainly to the Jews; see Léon Vignols, *Le commerce hollandais et les congrégations juives à la fin du XVII⁰ siècle* (*Revue historique*, 1890, vol. XLIV, p. 327–330).

⁶ It should be remarked that the Bank of Amsterdam was not the first example of an exchange bank with the character of a state bank. The Bank of St. George (*Banco di S. Giorgio*) had been founded at Genoa as early as the beginning of the fifteenth century (see H. Sieveking, *Genueser Finanzwesen*, Leipzig, 1899). At Venice, the *Banco di Rialto* had been formed toward the end of the Middle Ages; then, in 1619, there was founded a second state bank, the *Banco del Giro*. At Hamburg, the economic importance of which grew notably in the seventeenth century, an important exchange bank was founded in 1619. This remained in business until the nineteenth century (*cf.* Ernest H. Levy, *Die Hamburger Giro Bank und ihr Ausgang*, Berlin, 1890). On all the preceding, see the interesting study by J. B. van Dillen, *De girobanken van Genua, Venetië, en Hamburg* (*Tijdschrift voor Geschiedenis*, 1927).

⁷ On all the preceding, see also the *Mémoire sur le négoce et la navigation des Hollandais*, of Izaak Loysen, published by Petrus J. Blok, p. 307 *et seq.*, and especially the great collection of documents by J. G. van Dillen on the Dutch banks. *Cf.* C. Mees, *Proeve eener geschiedenis van het bankwezen in Nederland gerudende den tijd der Republik*, Rotterdam, 1836; and for a discussion in English see the chapter on the Bank of Amsterdam, in the earlier editions of Charles F. Dunbar: *Chapters on the Theory and History of Banking*, 1st ed., New York, 1891.

⁸ The London Company was given the exclusive right to plant the first settlement between 34 and 38 degrees of north latitude; the Plymouth Company the exclusive right to plant a colony between 41 and 45 degrees north. See Professor Edward Channing's *History of the United States*, vol. I., p. 157 *et seq.*

[9] *Stock* implies the idea of merchandise; *capital* is a financial security.

[10] At the same time, the dividends of the Dutch Company were only 166 per cent, but its capital was five times greater than that of the English Company. Naturally this rate per cent is calculated on the original capital of the shares.

[11] See Eugen Philippovitch, *Die Bank von England im Dienste der Finanzverwaltung des Staates*, Vienna, 1885, translated as *History of the Bank of England, National Monetary Commission*, Washington, 1911; John Sinclair, *History of the Public Revenue of the British Empire*, London, 1785; A. Andréadès, *History of the Bank of England*, London, 1909. By the seventeenth century, and especially at the time of the restoration of the Stuarts, use was made of fiduciary money and bank bills; and the use of checks also began to spread. See R. D. Richards, *The Evolution of Paper Money in England, The Quarterly Journal of Economics*, May, 1927.

[12] By the Edict of December 5, 1664, Colbert permitted gentlemen to carry on ocean commerce without losing their place in the nobility; the Edict of August 1669 declares: "We desire that a gentleman shall have the right to participate in a company and take a share in merchant vessels, so long as he does not sell at retail."

[13] In the first half of the seventeenth century, the trade of Nantes and Bordeaux was largely in the hands of foreigners, notably the Dutch. *Cf.* H. Sée, *Le commerce des étrangers et notamment des Hollandais, à Nantes pendant la minorité de Louis XIV* (*Tijdschrift voor geschiedenis*, 1926). On this subject, the most important document is Jean Eon, *Le commerce honorable*, Nantes, 1646.

[14] Above all the Dutch aimed at destroying the French trade. See G. N. Clark, *The Dutch Alliance and the War Against French Trade* (1688–1697), Manchester, 1923.

[15] From 1660 to 1672 there was complaint that the commercial balance worked to the advantage of France. *Cf.* W. J. Ashley, *The Tory Origins of Free Trade* (*Surveys Economic and Historic*), London, 1900.

[16] After using English and Dutch adventurers, Spain granted exclusive privileges in the slave trade to the French Guinea Company (*Compagnie française de Guinée*) in 1701. See Georges Scelle, *Histoire politique de la traite négrière aux Indes de Castille* (2 vols.), Paris, 1906.

¹⁷ See the excellent work of S. L. Mims, *Colbert's West India Policy* (*Yale Historical Studies*), New Haven, 1912.

¹⁸ This is demonstrated by Germain Martin and M. Bezançon in their remarkable work: *Histoire du crédit en France sous le règne de Louis XIV*, Paris, 1913.

CHAPTER VI

¹ It should be noted that the boats remained very small in size, an average of 100 tons.

² In 1710, imports represented only one-fifteenth part of consumption; cf. John Hobson, *The Evolution of Modern Capitalism*, London, 1894, p. 12–13.

³ Most of the industrial establishments at Nantes owed their beginnings to maritime commerce; and the cotton industry of Upper Normandy developed as a result of the stimulus received through the port of Rouen, (cf. J. Levainville, *Rouen*, Paris, 1913). At Rotterdam, in the eighteenth century, most of the industries (refineries, distilleries, etc.) developed out of the trade of this transit port; cf. Visser, *Verkeersindustrieen te Rotterdam in de tweede helft der XVIII eeuw*, Rotterdam, 1927. The author attributes to them a "protocapitalistic" character, i.e., he suggests that they represent an early stage in capitalistic enterprise.

⁴ Cf. Edwin Cannan, *A History of the Theories of Production and Distribution in English Political Economy*, 3rd ed., London, 1924; and L. L. Price, *A Short History of Political Economy in England from Adam Smith to Arnold Toynbee*, London, 1891.

⁵ This is shown by the following table:

	Bank of England	East India Company	South Sea Company	African Company
June-August	265	449	1020	200
December	132	145	121	45

⁶ On the preceding, see W. R. Scott, *op. cit.*, vol. I; and Lewis Melville (Lewis S. Benjamin), *The South Sea Bubble*, London, 1921.

⁷ It should be noted that the stock exchanges do not go farther back than the end of the seventeenth century; they are very different in-

stitutions from the old *bourses*, where the operations had to do mainly
with exchange and commercial transactions.

⁸ It was possible to secure insurance on a variety of contingencies at
this time. Thus, for example, it was possible to secure insurance on
marriages. In such cases, the policy-holders paid a certain sum every
week; and those of them who were married at a certain date, had the
premiums received divided amongst them and they then retired from
the society. There were also offices that insured a sum payable on
the christening of a child born in wedlock to a member. W. R. Scott,
Joint Stock Companies to 1720, vol. III, Cambridge, 1911, p. 369–
370.

⁹ Daniel DeFoe (*A Tour through Great Britain*, Cassell edition,
1898, p. 145 *et seq.*) notes that a packet service established between the
ports of Cornwall and Lisbon was transporting a great deal of gold
destined for London. See also Bento Carqueja, *O capitalismo moderno
e as suas origens em Portugal*, Oporto, 1908.

¹⁰ See Henri Weber, *La Compagnie des Indes Orientales*, Paris, 1904.
A new *Compagnie des Indes* was founded at the end of the *Ancien
Régime*.

¹¹ See, for example, the letters of the Abbé Tamisier to Cardinal
Gualterio, in 1719 and 1720, published in the *Mémoires de Saint-Simon*,
edited by A. de Boislisle, vol. 37 (1925), p. 486.

¹² See some exact data in H. Sée, *Le commerce de Saint-Malo au
XVIIIᵉ siècle*, (*Mémoires et documents pour servir à l'histoire du com-
merce*, published under the direction of Julien Hayem, 9th series,
Paris, 1925).

¹³ There were, however, important French banks like the establishment of Le Couteulx. Commercial correspondence furnished us with
considerable data in this respect. *Cf.* H. Sée, *Le commerce de Saint-
Malo au XVIIIᵉ siècle, op cit.*

¹⁴ See the edict establishing the *Bourse* in Richard Ehrenberg, *Das
Zeitalter der Fugger*, vol. II, p. 352 *et seq.;* these regulations were
reproduced in the patent of 1771 establishing the Vienna *Bourse*.

¹⁵ In 1720, a maritime insurance company (*Compagnie d'assurances
maritimes*) had been created at Hamburg; *cf.* C. Amsinck, *Die Erste
hamburgische Assecuranz-Compagnien und der Actienhandel im Jahren
1720 (Zeitschrift des Vereins für hamburgische Geschichte*, vol. IX,
p. 465 *et seq.*)

[16] This Company turned a quarter of its profits over to the king for the maintenance of a corps of firemen at Paris.

[17] See, for example, Henri Sée on the commerce of St.-Malo (*Le commerce de Saint-Malo au XVIIIe siècle, op. cit.*). Cf. Théophile Malvezin, *Histoire du commerce de Bordeaux*, Bordeaux, 1892; Georges Cirot, *Recherches sur les Juifs portugais et espagnols de Bordeaux*, Bordeaux, 1908 (from *Bulletin hispanique*) and *Les Juifs de Bordeaux, leur situation morale et sociale de 1550 à 1789*, 1920 from *Revue historique de Bordeaux*. Cf. Izak Prins, *De vestiging der Marranen in Noord-Nederland in de zestiende eeuw*, Amsterdam, 1927. The author shows that, by the sixteenth century, the Portuguese Jews were playing an important economic rôle in the Low Countries of the North.

[18] It has been shown by Hermann Wätjen that—except in the case of Brazil—Sombart has somewhat exaggerated the rôle played by the Jews in colonization (*Das Judentum und die Anfänge der Kolonization*, in the *Vierteljahrschrift für Social-und Wirtschaftsgeschichte*, 1913).

[19] On this subject very valuable data are contained in the work by Georges Cirot, *Les Juifs de Bordeaux, leur situation morale et sociale,* Bordeaux, 1920. See also H. Sée, *Note sur le commerce des Juifs en Bretagne au XVIIIe siècle* (*Revue des Etudes juives*, 1925).

[20] François Isambert, *Anciennes lois françaises*, vol. XXVIII, p. 246–248. There is also a *Déclaration* of March 19, 1786, which orders that all the commission business of the agents of Paris shall be carried on in particular places (to the number of 60), a measure caused by "the extent of commerce and the importance of the negotiations now carried on in our capital" (*Ibid.*, vol. XXVIII, p. 151–156).

[21] Articles *Paper Credit* and *Moneyed Interests*. This *Dictionary* was based directly upon that of Savary.

[22] Rennes was one of the provincial towns in which weekly *Affiches* were created (the *Affiches de Rennes* date from 1784). They contained but few commercial advertisements, however. Cf. H. Sée, *Les Affiches de Rennes* (*Annales historiques de la Révolution française*, 1926).

CHAPTER VII

[1] As shown by J. G. van Dillen in his paper on Amsterdam as a world market in the precious metals (in Dutch), *De Economist*, 1923; summarized in the *Revue historique*, 1926.

[2] The quotation in the text appears at p. 153 of vol. I of the edition of 1759, and at p. 107-8 in the edition of 1744. On the general subject of American commercial history, see Emory R. Johnson, *History of the Domestic and Foreign Commerce of the United States* (Carnegie Institution), Washington, 1915, vol. I, p. 36 *et seq.;* the several volumes by George L. Beer cited in the Bibliography; and C. L. Becker, *Beginning of the American People*, Boston, 1914.

[3] On this general subject, see Victor S. Clark, *History of Manufactures in the United States* (Carnegie Institution), Washington, 1916, and Carroll D. Wright, *Industrial Evolution in the United States*, New York, 1901.

[4] This point is well made by Charles M. Andrews, *The American Revolution, an historic interpretation (American Historical Review,* January, 1926).

[5] See Arthur M. Schlesinger, *The Colonial Merchants and the American Revolution* (Columbia University Studies in History, 1918); C. H. Van Tyne, *The Causes of the War of Independence*, New York, 1922; H. E. Egerton, *The Causes and Character of the American Revolution*, Oxford, 1923; Herbert L. Osgood, *The American Colonies in the Eighteenth Century*, New York, 1924-1925, 4 vol.; H. Hauser, *De quelques aspects de la Révolution américaine (La Révolution française,* 1921, vol. 74); James T. Adams, *Revolutionary New England*, Boston, 1923.

[6] This is from page 67 of the 1701 edition of a pamphlet attributed to Henry Martyn by P. J. Thomas, *Mercantilism and the East India Trade*, London, 1926.

CHAPTER VIII

[1] On this point, see the interesting observations of Charles Ballot, especially with reference to the silk industry (*L'introduction du machinisme*, Paris, 1923, p. 300 *et seq.*). The difference between institutions and customs must also be taken into account: England was not a centralized country like France, and Englishmen were not accustomed to look to the government for guidance and help.

[2] See W. J. Ashley, *Economic Organization of England*, p. 140 *et seq.;* E. Lipson, *History of the Woolen and Worsted Industries*, London, 1921; Herbert Heaton, *Yorkshire Worsted and Woolen Industries*, Oxford, 1920; Abel Chevalley, *Le roman des métiers au temps de*

Shakespeare, Paris, 1926. See Malachy Postlethwayt, *Universal Dictionary of Trade and Commerce*, London, 1751–1755, article on "Manufacturers," for a discussion of the legislation which provided penalties to be assessed against such artisans as might be guilty of appropriating raw materials,—further evidence of the character of the economic and business organization of the times.

[3] These seem to have been the outstanding features of the Irish linen industry, as disclosed in the recent work of Conrad Gill, *The Rise of the Irish Linen Industry*, Oxford, 1925.

[4] This is shown in Justin Godart's excellent volume, *L'ouvrier en soie de Lyon*, Lyons, 1899.

[5] Perhaps also the advantages in marketing contributed to the transformation of the scattered rural industry into the concentrated industry. For example, in Ireland the linen bleachers who exported direct to the great port of Liverpool, transformed themselves into industrial owners at the beginning of the nineteenth century (see Conrad Gill, *The Rise of the Irish Linen Industry*, Oxford, 1925); while the linen merchants of Laval—even such as were also bleachers—did not, on the other hand, become captains of industry. They possessed no direct outlet for their cloth. See H. Sée, *Le commerce des toiles dans le Bas-Maine dans la première moitié du XVIII° siècle, Mémoires et documents pour servir l'histoire du commerce et de l'industrie en France*, published under the direction of Julien Hayem, 10th series, Paris, 1926.

[6] See H. Sée, *A propos du mot "industrie"* (*Revue historique*, May 1925); H. Hauser, *Le mot "industrie" chez Roland de la Platière* (*Ibid.*, November, 1925).

[7] In his introduction to Henry Hamilton, *The Copper and Brass Industries of England to 1800*, London, 1926.

[8] The economic work of Adam Smith gives us the impression that at the time he was writing the *Wealth of Nations* (1776), the industrial transformation was only then beginning. He opposes the regulations, pronounces himself in favor of economic liberty and division of labor; but the problems with which he deals are less complicated than they would have been, had the evolution been farther along.

CHAPTER IX

[1] *An Economic History of Modern Britain: The Early Railway Age (1820–1850)*, Cambridge, 1926. Professor Clapham makes very happy use of the census reports.

[2] In Faucigny, the clock industry has preserved its family character until the twentieth century; the mountaineers devote their long winter leisure to this manufacture. See A. Cholley, *Les Préalpes de Savoie*, Paris, 1925.

[3] As is shown by the *Enquête du Comité du travail*, in 1848. The situation in Paris in 1851 is shown by the *Statistique de la Chambre de commerce*, of 1851.

[4] It should be noted, however, that roads were being improved and that main highways and local roads were being constructed.

[5] See H. Sée, *L'évolution du régime agraire en Angleterre* (*Revue de synthèse historique*, December 1924); J. L. and B. Hammond, *The Village Labourer*, 4th ed., London, 1927; Lord Ernle, *English Farming Past and Present*, 4th ed., London, 1927.

[6] This is shown very clearly by Eugène Schkaff's book: *La question agraire en Russie*, Paris, 1922; and see James Mavor, *Economic History of Russia*, 2nd ed., London and New York, 1925.

[7] N. S. B. Gras, *A History of Agriculture in Europe and America*, New York, 1925. Today, on the contrary, there is no country where agriculture is more influenced by commercial markets and capitalism.

CHAPTER X

[1] This, at least, is what is shown by the latest works published on this subject—works which correct the somewhat one-sided theories of Salvemini, Davidsohn, and Caggese in singular fashion. See, for example, Volpe, *Medio evo italiano*, Florence, 1923; N. Ottokar, *Il commune di Firenze alla fine del dugento*, Florence, 1926; Federico Chabod, *Die alcuni studi recenti sull 'età communale e signorile nell' Italia settentrionale* (*Rivista storica italiana*, January, 1925).

[2] The levy of the indirect taxes on merchandise (*aides*) and on salt (*gabelle*) provoked popular riots, especially at Paris (the *Maillotins*) and in some other cities, notably at Rouen (1381). In the South, in Languedoc, bands of poor ruined people overran the country, pillaging wherever they could (1382–1384). These disorders were harshly repressed; see Léon Mirot, *Les émeutes parisiennes de 1380–1383* (*Mémoire de la Société de l'Histoire de Paris*, Vol. 28, 1901); Boudet, *La Jacquerie des Tuchins*, 1895.

[3] For all the following, see Henri Sée, *L'évolution du régime agraire en Angleterre* (*Revue de synthèse historique*, December 1924); Lord

Ernle, *English Farming, Past and Present*, 4th ed., London, 1927.

[4] See R. H. Tawney, *The Agrarian Problem in the Sixteenth Century*, London, 1912. In the Low Countries, in the sixteenth century, capitalism also filters into agricultural life. A system of farm rents develops and a proletariat class comes into being. See Henri Pirenne, *Histoire de Belgique*, vol. III, p. 256–258.

[5] Louis Moffit, *England on the Eve of the Industrial Revolution*, London, 1925. Professor J. H. Clapham (*An Economic History of Modern Britain*) has also shown that, in the period 1815 to 1850, the small holding had by no means completely disappeared.

[6] *The Complete English Tradesman*, Letter XXII, first ed., London, 1726, p. 376. It is interesting to note also that the agrarian evictions and the depopulation of the country had the effect of setting up a considerable emigration, which contributed toward the colonial expansion.

[7] These facts have been brought to light by J. Rutkowski in an important work (in Polish) on *The Problem of Agricultural Reform in Poland in the Eighteenth Century*, Posen, 1925. See also J. Rutkowski, *Histoire économique de la Pologne*, translated from the Polish, Paris, 1927.

[8] It should be noted that in the eighteenth century the Physiocrats, upholders of the system of large properties, were also in favor of the abolition of serfdom and the manorial dues; the same is true of Arthur Young (*Travels in France*, various editions, *passim*).

[9] Thus, the Laval linen merchants, in the eighteenth century, bought lands and contracted alliances with the old nobility. *Cf.* J. M. Richard, *La vie privée dans une province de l'Ouest: Laval aux XII* et XIII* siècles*, Paris, 1922.

[10] Elie Halévy, *Histoire du peuple anglais*, vol. III, pp. 305–306; and see also J. H. Clapham, *op. cit.* Professor Clapman calls attention to the fact that the cost of living fell by about 30 per cent from 1820 to 1850, whereas the level of wages remained practically unchanged.

[11] On Chartism, see Mark Hovell, *The Chartist Movement*, Manchester, 1918; the briefer discussion in A. P. Usher, *The Industrial History of England*, Boston, 1920, p. 512–518; and especially the fascinating *Life of Francis Place*, 1771–1854, by Graham Wallas, London, 1898.

[12] See Henri Sée, *Matérialisme historique et interprétation économique de l'histoire*, Paris, 1927, English Edition, New York, 1928; *cf.* also Henri de Man, *Au delà du Marxisme*, Brussels, 1927.

CHAPTER XI

[1] It should be noted further, that today—especially since the World War—financial capitalism has tended to outdistance industrial capitalism, which, in certain cases, now seems to play only a subordinate rôle. This at least is the contention of Thorstein Veblen, *Absentee Ownership and Business Enterprise in Recent Times; the Case of America*, New York, 1923. As Arturo Labriola says in *Il capitalismo*, Turin, 1910, p. 275 *et seq.*, "capitalism returns to the sphere of circulation." *Cf.* also Werner Sombart, *Das Wirtschaftsleben im Zeitalter des Hochkapitalismus*, Munich, 1927; and E. Teilhac, *L'évolution juridique des trusts et sa portée*, Paris, 1927.

[2] The commercial relations of Venice, Genoa, Pisa, and Florence with the Orient, particularly intense after the Crusades, not only contributed to the accumulation of capital, from which the first development of capitalism proceeds; they also reacted indirectly on Italian thought and art. See A. Renaudet, *Les influences orientales dans la "Divine Comédie" et dans la peinture toscane* (*Revue de synthèse historique*, December, 1925).

[3] See the suggestive article by Haldvan Koht, *Le problème des origines de la Renaissance* (*Revue de synthèse historique*, June, 1914).

BIBLIOGRAPHY

A complete bibliography would necessarily include most works relating to economic history; that which follows suggests those most interesting and most useful in tracing the evolution of capitalism. More specialized and detailed bibliographies are to be found in many of the volumes listed below, notably those of W. J. Ashley, Edward Channing, William Cunningham, Clive Day, M. M. Knight, and A. P. Usher. An elaborate critical bibliography on the Industrial Revolution has recently been prepared by Eileen Power and published by the Economic History Society: *The Industrial Revolution, a Select Bibliography*, Oxford, 1927.

Abbott, Frank F. *The Common People of Ancient Rome*, New York, 1911.

Abbott, W. C. *The Expansion of Europe; a Social and Political History of the Modern World, 1415–1789* (2 vols.), London, 1925.

Andréadès, A. *History of the Bank of England*, London, 1909.

Andrews, Charles M. *The Colonial Background of the American Revolution*, New Haven, 1924.

Ashley, William J. *An Introduction to English Economic History and Theory* (2 vols.), London and New York, 1888–1893; *The Economic Organization of England*, London and New York, 1914; 8th ed., 1924; translated into French as *L'évolution économique de l'Angleterre*, Paris, 1926.

Ashton, Thomas Southcliffe. *Iron and Steel in the Industrial Revolution*, London, 1924.

Augé-Laribé, Michel. *L'évolution agricole de la France*, Paris, 1912.

Baasch, Ernst. *Die holländische Wirtschaftsgeschichte*, Jena, 1927. (Brodnitz collection.)

Ballot, Charles. *L'introduction du machinisme dans l'industrie française (Comité des travaux historiques, section d'histoire moderne et contemporaine)*, Paris, 1923.

Beer, George L. *Organization of the British Colonial System, 1578–1660*, New York, 1908;—*British Colonial Policy, 1754–1765*, New York, 1907;—*The Old Colonial System* (2 vols.), New York, 1912.

Benjamin, Lewis S. (Louis Melville.) *The South Sea Bubble*, London, 1921.

Bensa, Enrico. *Il contratto di assicurazione nel medio ero*, Genoa, 1884.

Bigwood, Georges. *Le régime juridique et économique de l'argent en Belgique au moyen âge* (*Mémoires de l'Académie de Belgique*, 1921– 1922) ;—*Les financiers d'Arras* (*Revue belge de philologie et d'histoire*, 1924–1925).

Blok, Petrus J. *History of the People of the Netherlands* (5 vols.), New York and London, 1912, a translation of *Geschiedenis van het Nederlandsch volk* (8 vols.), Groningen, 1892–1908; Editor: *Mémoire touchant le commerce et la navigation des Hollandais*, by Izaak Loysen, 1699 (*Bijdragen van het historisch genootschap*, No. XXIV, The Hague).

Bober, M. M. *Karl Marx's Interpretation of History* (Harvard Economic Studies), Cambridge, 1927.

Boissourrade, P. *Le socialisme d'Etat, les classes industrielles en France pendant les deux premiers siècles de l'ère moderne* (*1453– 1661*), Paris, 1927.

Bonfaute, P. *Lezioni di storia del commercio*, Rome, 1925.

Bonnassieux, Pierre. *Les grandes compagnies de commerce*, Paris, 1892.

Bonzon, Alfred. *La banque à Lyon, aux XVI', XVII' et XVIII' siècle* (*Revue d'histoire de Lyon*, 1902 and 1903).

Bouglé, Charles. *Revue générale des théories récentes relatives à la division du travail* (*Année sociologique*, 6th year, 1901–1902, pp. 73– 133).

Bourdais, F. and Durand, René. *L'industrie et le commerce de la toile en Bretagne au XVIII' siècle*, 1922 (*Comité des travaux historiques, section d'histoire moderne et contemporaine*, No. VII).

Bowden, Witt. *Industrial Society in England towards the End of the Eighteenth Century*, New York, 1925.

Burgon, John W. *Life and Times of Sir Thomas Gresham*, London, 1839.

Bourquelot, Felix. *Etudes sur les foires de Champagne* (*Mémoires présentés à l'Académie des Inscriptions*), 1865.

Brakel, S. van. *Die holländsche handelscompagnieen der zeventiende eeuw*, The Hague, 1908.

Brentano, L. *Die Anfänge des modernen Kapitalismus*, Munich, 1916.

Calhoun, George. *Business Life of Ancient Athens*, Chicago, 1926.

Carqueja, Bento. *A capitalismo moderno e as suas origens em Portugal*, Oporto, 1908.

Channing, Edward. *The History of the United States* (6 vols. published thus far), New York, 1907–.

Chlepner, B. S. *La banque en Belgique*, Brussels, 1926.

Cirot, Georges. *Les Juifs de Bordeaux; leur situation morale et sociale de 1550 à 1789*, Bordeaux, 1920 (from the *Revue historique de Bordeaux*).

Clapham, J. H. *The Economic Development of France and Germany* (1815–1914), Cambridge, 1921;—*An Economic History of Modern Britain; the Early Railway Age, 1820–1850*, Cambridge, 1926.

Clark, Victor S. *History of Manufactures in the United States, 1607–1860*, Carnegie Institution, Washington, 1916.

Cleveland-Stevens, Edward. *English Railways*, London, 1915.

Coulton, G. *The Medieval Village*, Cambridge, 1925.

Courtois, Alph. *Histoire des banques en France*, Paris, 1881.

Cunningham, William. *The Growth of English Industry and Commerce* (6th ed.), Cambridge, 1915–1919.

d'Avenel, Georges. *Histoire économique de la propriété, des salaires, des denrées et des prix de l'an 1200 à l'an 1800*, 5 vol., Paris, 1894–1926.

Dahlgren, E. W. *Les relations commerciales et maritimes entre la France et les côtes de l'Océan Pacifique*, Paris, 1909.

Datz, Paul. *Histoire de la publicité*, Paris, 1894.

Davidsohn, Robert. *Geschichte von Florenz* (4 vols.), Berlin, 1896–1927;—*Forschungen zur Geschichte von Florenz*, Berlin, 1896–1908.

Davis, Joseph S. *Essays in the Earlier History of American Corporations* (Harvard Economic Studies), Cambridge, 1917.

Davis, William Stearns, *The Influence of Wealth in Imperial Rome*, New York, 1910;—*Life on a Medieval Barony*, New York, 1923.

Day, Clive. *A History of Commerce*, New York, 1907; revised ed., 1922.

Demangeon, Albert. *L'Empire britannique*, Paris, 1923;—*La Picardie et les régions voisines*, Paris, 1905.

des Marez, G. *La lettre de foire à Ypres au XIII* siècle*, Brussels,

1901;—*L'organisation du travail à Bruxelles au XV* siècle*, Brussels, 1904.

Dillen, J. G. van. *Bronnen tot de geschiedenis der Wisselbanken* (*Amsterdam, Middelburg, Delft, Rotterdam*) (2 vols.), The Hague, 125;—*Amsterdam, a World Market for the Precious Metals in the XVIIth and XVIIIth Centuries* (in Dutch), *De Economist*, 1923, (summarized in the *Revue historique*, July, 1926).

Dopsch, Alfons. *Wirtschaftliche und soziale Grundlagen der europaeischen Kulturentwickelung* (2 vols.), Vienna, 1918–1920.

Doren, Alfred. *Studien aus der Florentiner Wirtschaftsgeschichte*, Stuttgart, 1901;—*Das Florentiner Zunftwesen vom XIVten Jahrhundert zum XVIten*, Stuttgart, 1908.

Edmundson, George. *Anglo-Dutch Rivalry during the First Half of the Seventeenth Century*, Oxford, 1911.

Ehrenberg, Richard. *Das Zeitalter der Fugger* (2 vols.), Jena, 1896.

Encyclopédie départementale des Bouches-du-Rhône, published under the direction of Paul Masson, vols. VIII, IX, and X, Marseilles, 1922–1925.

Ernle, Lord. *English Farming, Past and Present*, 4th ed., London 1927.

Espinas, Georges. *L'industrie dans la Flandre française au moyen âge*, Paris, 2 vols., 1923.

Fagniez, Gustave. *Études sur l'industrie et la classe industrielle à Paris aux XIIIe et XIVe siècles* (Library of the *École des Hautes Études*, No. 33), Paris, 1877;—*Documents relatifs à l'histoire de l'industrie et du commerce en France au moyen âge* (2 vols.), Paris, 1898–1900;—*L'économie sociale de la France sous Henri IV*, Paris, 1897.

Faulkner, Harold U. *American Economic History*, New York, 1924.

Festy, O. *Le mouvement ouvrier au début de la monarchie de juillet* (1830–1834), Paris, 1908.

Forbonnais, F. V. D. de. *Recherches et considérations sur les finances de France* (2 vols.), Basle, 1758.

Francotte, Henri. *L'industrie dans la Grèce ancienne* (*Société belge de librairie*), Brussels, 1900.

Frank, Tenney. *An Economic History of Rome*, 2nd ed., Baltimore, 1927.

Génestal, R. *Rôle des monastères comme établissements de crédit*, *étudié en Normandie du XI*^e *à la fin du XIII*^e *siècle*, Paris, 1901.

Gill, Conrad. *The Rise of the Irish Linen Industry*, Oxford, 1925.

Godart, Justin. *L'ouvrier en soie de Lyon*, Lyons, 1901.

Goris, J. A. *Les colonies méridionales à Anvers de 1488 à 1567* (Publication of the University of Louvain), Louvain, 1925.

Gras, N. S. B. *A History of Agriculture in Europe and America*, New York, 1925.

Guiccardini, Lodovico. *Descrittioni di tutti Paesi Bassi*, Antwerp, 1567.

Guiraud, Paul. *La main-d'œuvre industrielle dans l'ancienne Grèce*, Paris, 1900.

Halévy, Élie. *Histoire du peuple anglais au XIX*^e *siècle* (3 vols.), Paris, 1913–1923; vol. I translated as *A History of the English People in 1815*, New York, 1924.

Hamilton, Henry. *The English Brass and Copper Industries to 1800*, London, 1926.

Haring, Clarence H. *Trade and Navigation between Spain and Indies under the Hapsburgs* (Harvard Economic Studies), Cambridge, 1918.

Hauser, Henri. *Travailleurs et marchands de l'ancienne France*, Paris, 1920;—*Ouvriers du temps passé*, Paris, 1899;—*Les origines du capitalisme moderne en France* (*Revue d'économie politique*, 1902); —*Le mot "industrie" chez Roland de la Platière* (*Revue historique*, November, 1925);—*Le parfait négociant de Jaques Savary*, Paris, 1924;—*Les débuts du capitalisme*, Paris, 1927 (a collection of the foregoing essays);—*Spéculation et spéculateurs au XVI*^e *siècle* (in *Travailleurs et marchands de l'ancienne France*, Paris, 1920).

Heaton, Herbert. *Yorkshire Woolen and Worsted Industries*, Oxford, 1920.

Hodgson, F. C. *Venice in the Thirteenth and Fourteenth Centuries*, London, 1910.

Horsburgh, E. L. S. *Lorenzo the Magnificent*, London, 1908.

Hottenger, Georges. *La Lorraine économique au lendemain de la Révolution, d'après les mémoires statistiques des préfets le l'an IX*, Nancy, 1924.

Huet, P. D. *Mémoires sur le commerce des Hollandais*, Amsterdam, 1717 and 1718; translated as *Memoirs of the Dutch Trade in all the States, Kingdoms, and Empires in the World*, London (1700 ca.).

Huvelin, Paul. *Essai historique sur le droit des marchés et des foires*, Paris, 1897;—*Le droit commercial* (*Revue de synthèse historique*, 1904, vol. VIII, p. 198–243).

Johnson, Emory R. *Domestic and Foreign Commerce of the United States*, Carnegie Institution, Washington, 1915.

Klerk de Reuss, G. C. *Geschichtlicher Ueberblick der administrativen, rechtlichen und finanziellen Entwickelung der niederlandischen Ostindischen Companie*, The Hague, 1894.

Kletler, Paul. *Nordwesteuropas Verkehr, Handel und Gewerbe*, Vienna, 1924.

Kluchevsky, V. O. *A History of Russia*, London, 1911.

Knight, Melvin M. *Economic History of Europe to the End of the Middle Ages*, Boston, 1926.

Knowles, L. C. A. *The Industrial and Commercial Revolutions in Great Britain during the Nineteenth Century*, London and New York, 1921.

Kulischer, Josef. *Russische Wirtschaftsgeschichte*, Jena, 1921 (Brodnitz Collection);—*Warenhändler und Geldausleiher im Mittelalter* (*Zeitschrift für Volkswirtschaft, Sozialpolitik und Verwaltung*, vol. XVII).

Kuske, Bruno. *Die Enstehung der Kreditwirtschaft und des Kapitalverkehrs*, Leipzig, 1927.

Labriola, A. *Il capitalismo; lineamenti storici*, 2nd ed., Naples, 1926.

Lavene, Ricardo. *Comercio de Indias* (*Documentos para la historia argentina*) (3 vols.), Buenos Aires, 1916.

Lefebre, Georges. *Les paysans du Nord pendant la Révolution française*, Lille, 1924.

Leroy-Beaulieu, Paul. *La colonisation chez les peuples modernes*, 6th ed., Paris, 1908.

Levasseur, Emile, *Histoire des classes ouvrieres et de l'industrie en France avant 1789*, 2nd ed. (2 vols.), Paris 1901;—*Histoire des classes ouvrières en France de 1789 à 1870*, 2nd ed. (2 vols.), Paris, 1903–1904;—*Histoire du commerce de la France* (2 vols.), Paris, 1911;—*Recherches historiques sur le système de Law*, 1854.

Levy, Robert. *Histoire économique de l'industrie cotonnière en Alsace*, Paris, 1912.

Lipson, Ephraim. *History of the Woolen and Worsted Industries*, London, 1921; *An Introduction to the Economic History of England*, vol. 1, 4th ed., London, 1926.

Lot, Ferdinand. *La fin du monde antique et le début du moyen âge*, Paris, 1928.

Lucas, C. P. *The Beginnings of the English Overseas Empire*, Oxford, 1917.

Luzac, Elie. *Holland's Rijkdom (Holland's Wealth)*, a translation, with additions, of a work by Accarias de Sérionne, published in London in 1778, under the French title *Commerce de la Hollande*, Amsterdam, 1778.

Mantoux, Paul. *La révolution industrielle au XVIIIe siècle*, Paris, 1905; English edition, New York, 1928.

Marion, M. *Dictionnaire des institutions de la France aux XVIIe et XVIIIe siècles*, Paris, 1923, articles on *ferme générale, receveurs généraux, rentes, traitants, trésoriers.*

Martin, Germain. *La grande industrie en France sous le règne de Louis XIV*, Paris, 1899;—*La grande industrie en France sous le règne de Louis XV*, Paris, 1900;—*La monnaie et le crédit privé en France aux XVIIe et XVIIIe siècles (Revue d'histoire des doctrines économiques*, vol. II, 1909).

Martin, Germain and Bezançon, Marcel. *Histoire du crédit en France sous le règne de Louis XIV*, Paris, 1913.

Martin-Saint-Léon, Etienne. *Histoire des corporations de métiers*, 3rd ed., Paris, 1923.

Marx, Karl. *Das Kapital*. Translated under the title *Capital* by Samuel Moore and Edward Aveling, Chicago, 1906.

Masson, Paul. *Histoire du commerce français dans le Levant au XVIIe siècle*, Paris, 1906;—*Histoire du commerce français dans le Levant au XVIIIe siècle*, Paris, 1911.

Mathiez, Albert. *La vie chère et le mouvement social sous la Terreur*, Paris, 1927.

Mayer, Georges. *Essai sur les origines du crédit en France du XIIIe au XIVe siècle*, Paris, 1902.

Mims, Stewart L. *Colbert's West India Policy* (Yale Historical Studies), New Haven, 1912.

Moffit, Louis. *England on the Eve of the Industrial Revolution* (1740–1760) *with special reference to Lancashire*, London, 1925.

Morison, S. E. *The Maritime History of Massachusetts*, Boston, 1921.

Naudé, Wilhelm. *Die Getreidehandelspolitik der europäischen Staaten vom XIIten bis zum XVIIIten Jahrhundert*, Berlin, 1896–1910.

Osgood, Herbert. *American Colonies in the Seventeenth Century*, New York, 1904–1907;—*American Colonies in the Eighteenth Century*, New York, 1924–1925.

Pasquet, D. *Histoire politique et sociale du peuple américain*, Paris, 1924.

Peruzzi, Simone L. *Storia del commercio e dei banchieri di Firenze in tutto il mondo conosciuto del 1200 al 1345*, Florence, 1868.

Phillips, Ulrich B. *American Negro Slavery*, New York, 1918.

Pigeonneau, Henri. *Histoire du commerce de la France* (2 vols.), Paris, 1887–1889.

Pirenne, Henri. *Histoire de Belgique* (5 vols.), Brussels, 1902–1926;—*Les anciennes démocraties des Pays-Bas*, Paris, 1910, translated as *Belgian Democracy; Its Early History*, Manchester, 1915;—*Les périodes de l'histoire sociale du capitalisme* (*Mémoires de l'Académie de Belgique*, Brussels, 1914).

Piton, Camille. *Les Lombards en France et à Paris*, Paris, 1892.

Power, Eileen. *Medieval People*, London, 1924; 3d ed., Boston, 1926.

Pringsheim, Otto. *Beiträge zur wirtschaftlichen Entwickelungsgeschichte der Vereinigten Niederlande im XVIIten und XVIIIten Jahrhundert*, 1890 (*Forschungen* of Schmoller, vol. X).

Raveau, Paul. *L'agriculture et les classes paysannes dans le Haut-Poitou au XVIe siècle*, Paris, 1925.

Ravignani, Emilio. *Historia Constitutional de la República Argentina*, Buenos Aires, 1926.

Renard, Georges François. *Histoire du travail à Florence* (2 vols.), Paris, 1914;—*Guilds in the Middle Ages*, London, 1918.

Rouff, Marcel. *Les mines de charbon en France au XVIIIe siècle*, 1744–1791; Paris, 1922.

Salter, F. R. *Sir Thomas Gresham*, 1518–1579, London and Boston, 1925.

Salvioli, Giuseppe. *Le capitalisme dans le monde antique*, translated into French, Paris, 1906.

Salzman, L. F. *English Industries of the Middle Ages*, Oxford, 1923.

Sampson, Henry. *History of Advertising*, London, 1875.

Savary, Jacques. *Le parfait négociant*, 1st ed., Paris, 1673, 7th ed., 1713.

Savary des Brulons, Jacques. *Dictionnaire universal de commerce*, 1738–1741 and 1759–1765, 5 vols., translated with additions by Malachy Postlethwayt, *The Universal Dictionary of Trade and Commerce*, London, 1751–5, 1757, 1766, 1774.

Sayous, André A. *Les charges de l'Espagne sur l'Amérique au XVIᵉ siècle (Revue d'économie politique*, 1927);—*Les procédés de paiement de la monnaie dans l'Amérique espagnole du XVIᵉ siècle (Revue économique internationale*, November, 1927).

Sayous, André E. *Les sociétés anonymes par actions (Revue d'économie politique*, July, 1902).

Scelle, Georges. *Histoire politique de la traite négrière aux Indes de Castille* (2 vols.), Paris, 1906.

Schanz, Georg. *Englische Handelspolitik gegen Ende des Mittelalters*, Leipzig, 1881.

Schevill, Ferdinand. *Siena, the Story of a Medieval Commune*, New York, 1909.

Schkaff, Eugène. *La question agraire en Russie*, Paris, 1922.

Schlesinger, Arthur M. *The Colonial Merchants and the American Revolution* (Columbia University Studies in History), New York, 1918.

Scott, William. R. *The Constitution and Finance of English, Scotch and Irish Joint Stock Companies to 1720* (3 vols.), Cambridge, 1910–12.

Sée, Henri. *L'évolution commerciale et industrielle de la France sous l'Ancien Régime*, Paris, 1925;—*La vie économique et les classes sociales en France au XVIIIᵉ siècle*, Paris, 1924; translated as *Economic and Social Conditions in France during the Eighteenth Century*, New York, 1927;—*Le commerce de Saint-Malo au XVIIIᵉ siècle (Mémoires et documents pour servir à l'histoire du commerce et de l'industrie en France*, published under the direction of Julien Hayem, 9th series, Paris, 1925);—*Le commerce des toiles dans le Bas-Maine dans la première moitié du XVIIIᵉ siècle*, and *Etudes sur le commerce et l'industrie au XVIIIᵉ siècle (Ibid.*, 10th series, Paris, 1926);—*Esquisse d'une histoire du régime agraire en Europe au XVIIIᵉ et XIXᵉ siècles*, Paris, 1921;—*La France économique et sociale au XVIIIᵉ siècle*, Paris, 1925 (Armand Colin Collection);—*La vie économique de la France sous la monarchie censitaire (1815–1848)*, Paris, 1927;—*Matérialisme historique et interprétation économique de l'histoire*, Paris, 1927;—*Notes sur les assurances maritimes en France, et particulièrement à*

Nantes, au XVIIIe siècle (*Revue historique du droit*, 1927);—*A propos du mot "industrie"* (*Revue historique*, 1925);—*L'activité commerciale de la Hollande à la fin du XVIIe siècle* (*Revue d'histoire économique*, 1926);—*Documents sur le commerce de Cadix* (*Revue de l'historie des colonies françaises*).

Selfridge, H. Gordon. *The Romance of Commerce*, London and New York, 1923.

Sombart, Werner. *Der moderne Kapitalismus*, 4th ed., 4 vols., 1922; —*The Jews and Modern Capitalism*, (a translation by M. Epstein) London, 1913;—*Der Bourgeois*, Leipzig, 1913, translated by M. Epstein as *The Quintessence of Capitalism*, London, 1915;—*Das Wirtschaftsleben im Zeitalter des Hochkapitalismus*, Munich, 1927.

Staley, Edgcumbe. *The Guilds of Florence*, London, 1906.

Strieder, Jakob. *Zur Genesis des modernen Kapitalismus*, Bonn, 1903, Leipzig, 1904;—*Studien zur Geschichte kapitalistischer Organisationsformen (Monopole, Kartelle und Aktiengesellschaften) im Mittelalter und zu Beginn der Neuzeit*, 2nd ed., Munich and Leipzig, 1925.

Tarlé, E. V. *L'industrie dans les campagnes en France à la fin de l'Ancien Régime*, Paris, 1910.

Tawney, Richard H. *The Agrarian Problem in the Sixteenth Century*, London and New York, 1912;—*Religion and the Rise of Capitalism*, London and New York, 1926.

Thirion, Henri. *Vie privée des financiers au XVIIIe siècle*, Paris, 1895.

Toynbee, Arnold. *Lectures on the Industrial Revolution*, London, 1884; new ed., 1927.

Trevelyan, George M. *British History in the Nineteenth Century*, London and New York, 1922.

Troeltsch, Ernst. *Die sozialen Lehren der christlichen Kirchen und Gruppen*, Tübingen, 1912.

Unwin, George. *The Industrial Organisation in the Sixteenth and Seventeenth Centuries*, 1904;—*Samuel Oldknow and the Arkwrights, the Industrial Revolution at Stockport and Marple*, London, 1924; —*Studies in Economic History*, London, 1927.

Usher, A. P. *An Introduction to the Industrial History of England*, Boston, 1920.

Vigne, Marcelin. *La banque à Lyon du XVe au XVIIIe siècle*, Paris and Lyons, 1903.

Vignols, Léon. *Le commerce interlope français à la mer du Sud au début du XVIIIᵉ siècle* (*Revue d'histoire économique*, 1925).

Villari, Pasquale. *The Two First Centuries of Florentine History*, London and New York, 1895.

von Halle, Ernst. *Die Baumwollproduktion und die Pflanzungswirtschaft in den nordamerikanischen Südstaaten* (*Forschungen* of Schmoller), Leipzig, 1897.

von Klarwill, Victor, (Ed.). *The Fugger News-Letters*, London and New York, 1924;—*Second Series*, 1926.

Walford, Cornelius. *Fairs, Past and Present*, London, 1883.

Weber, Henri. *La Compagnie des Indes Orientales*, Paris, 1904.

Weber, Max. *Die protestantische Ethik und der Geist der Kapitalismus*, 1904–1905 (reprinted in *Gesammelte Aufsätze zur Religionsoziologie*, Tübingen, 1920–1921);—*Allgemeine Wirtschaftsgeschichte*, translated into English as *General economic history* by Frank H. Knight, New York, 1927.

Wegg, Jervis. *Antwerp, 1477–1559*, London, 1916.

Wilson, Thomas. *A Discourse upon Usury* (1572), edited, with an excellent introduction, by R. H. Tawney, London, 1925.

Wright, Carroll D. *Industrial Evolution of the United States*, New York, 1901.

Yver, Georges. *Le commerce et les marchands dans l'Italie méridionale au XIIIᵉ et au XIVᵉ siècle*, Paris, 1903.

Zimmermann, Alfred. *Die Kolonialpolitik Grossbritanniens* (2 vols.), Berlin, 1898;—*Die Kolonialpolitik der Niederländer*, Berlin, 1903.

Zimmern, Helen. *The Hansa Towns*, New York, 1889.

INDEX OF NAMES

SUBJECT INDEX

136, 142, 143, 150, 154, 163, 167; industrial operations, 168, 169, 181. See "Putting-out" system

Insurance, in France, 15; maritime, 21, 31, 89, 91, 184; life, 89; fire, 89, 94, 95; corporation, 94, 197; *grosse aventure*, 184

Italy, capitalism, 2, 7, 9, 25; maritime commerce, 7; financial activity, 18, 29; commercial societies in Middle Ages, *Société en commandite, en nom collectif*, 20, 21, 78; cloth industry, 27; commerce in Spanish America, 49; cities, 157, 177; Italian republics, 157

Jamaica, 58; acquired by English in 1655, 67

Jennies, see Textile industry

Jews, influence on early capitalism in Spain, 18; international economic power, 22, 25; money lending, 28; expulsion of, 60, 96; influence on capital, 186

Joint stock companies, development of, 55, 56, 116, 142, 187, 193; *Société en commandite*, 20, 21, 78; in cotton industry, 134

Labor, in ancient world, 1, 4, 5; trade guilds in the Middle Ages, 24, 25; *asiento*, slave trade, 59, 67, 68, 193; shortage of, 108; system of division of, 135, 136; Ten Hour Law in 1847, 142; manorial system, 158; labor problems, 163, 166, 167, 169, 170; concentration, 181; capitalism as a function of, 183

Laissez-faire, 168

Landed property, 5; influence of capitalism on, 158

Languedoc, domestic trade of, 72; banking in, 80

Latifundia, 1

Lettre de foire, see Bill of exchange

Levant, 8, 15; French trade with, 74, 91, 93

Linen industry, see Textile industry

Liverpool, 86, 87, 118

Lombards, bankers, 9, 18, 22, 28; lombard-houses, 20

London, 85, 97

Louviers, 126, 130, 135, 143

Low Countries, in 13th century, origin, nature and influence of capitalism in, 2; first signs of capitalism in, 7; maritime commerce of, 7; geographical conditions, 10; founding of cities *(portus)*, 10; trading, 10; growth of population, 12; urban patriciate, effect on commercial expansion, 12; economic situation of episcopal cities, 12; Northern Low Countries, seat of commercial capitalism, 13; resources, 13; financiers, Crespins, Lombards, 18; capitalism, 25; cloth industry, 27, 157

Luddite movement, 168

Lyons, silk industry, 15, 124, 166; financial importance of, 29, 30; religion of, 40; bank of, 93, 145; commission houses in, 119, 126

Machinery, introduction of, 129, 134, 168; cotton, 130; demonstrations against, 168, 169, 181

Mainmorte, 6

Mamelukes of Egypt, 51

Manorial system, see Social structure

Manufacture, see Industry

Marans, converted Portuguese Jews, 29, 42

Marseilles, established as free port by Colbert, 74; merchants of, 91

Martinique, 58; trade of, 76

Marx, Karl, on factory system, 127; on evolution of capitalism, 155, 174; on social repercussions, 175; Marxian orthodoxy, 174, 175, 183, 184

Mercantilist policy in 17th century, 60, 61; Colbert's policy, 60; destruction of policy, 61, 128; system, 72-73; doctrines, 87; in English colonial policy, 104, 106, 109

Mercers, see Textile industry

Merchant Adventurers, 17, 18, 53, 55, 69

Merchants of 12th century, 11; of 15th century, 16

Merchant-manufacturer, functions of, 121-125, 134, 137, 140

Métayers, small or medium tenants, 160

Mining and metals, exploitation of mineral resources in 15th century, 28; precious metals of colonies, 44,